The Weekend Mechanic's
Auto Body Repair Guide

For our parents

The Weekend Mechanic's
Auto Body Repair Guide

*Robert Grossblatt and
Billy Boynton*

TAB BOOKS
Blue Ridge Summit, PA

Bondo®   **Dynatron/Bondo Corp.**

FIRST EDITION
FIRST PRINTING

© 1991 by **Robert Grossblatt and Billy Boynton**.
Published by TAB Books.
TAB Books is a division of McGraw-Hill, Inc.

Library of Congress Cataloging-in-Publication Data

Grossblatt, Robert.
    The weekend mechanic's auto body repair guide / by Robert
Grossblatt with Billy Boynton.
      p.   cm.
    Includes index.
    ISBN 0-8306-7497-7. — ISBN 0-8306-3497-5 (pbk.)
    1. Automobiles—Bodies—Maintenance and repair—Amateurs' manuals.
I. Boynton, Billy. II. Title.
TL255.G76 1990
629.24—dc20   90-21209
                                            CIP

TAB Books offers software for sale. For information and a catalog, please contact TAB Software Department, Blue Ridge Summit, PA 17294-0850.

Questions regarding the content of this book should be addressed to:

Reader Inquiry Branch
TAB Books
Blue Ridge Summit, PA 17294-0850

Acquisitions Editor: Kimberly Tabor
Book Editor: April D. Nolan
Production: Katherine G. Brown
Book Design: Jaclyn J. Boone
Cover photography: Brent Blair, Harrisburg, PA

Contents

Acknowledgments

Producing this book took a lot of time, work, and patience—lots and lots of patience. Even though no one was willing to do all the work for us (we know because we asked everyone we knew), there were a bunch of people who made the job much easier.

There's no way to thank everyone who helped us, but there are a few people who deserve mention because they threatened to kill us if they didn't see some form of their names in print. Therefore, in no particular order, we would like to extend our thanks to:

1. Richie and Mannie in the body shop. They not only helped but, believe it or not, refrained from laughing.
2. Walter, Eduardo, Juan, and George in the garage—who made it easier to keep the cars around and constantly offered us interesting suggestions, some of which even had to do with this book.
3. All the car owners who unwittingly allowed their vehicles to be photographed during a time they probably didn't want anyone to see them.
4. The people at TAB Books, particularly Kim Tabor, for all their patience, understanding, and willingness to answer what we now realize were incredibly stupid questions.

There are other people but there's some sort of rule about how the acknowledgments have to be shorter than the main text. These people know who they are and so do I. If anyone feels slighted, please call us and I promise to offer a personal apology.

Introduction

Life is made up of a series of milestones; they are the kinds of things you'll always remember. Some of them—your first step, your first word, or your first tooth—are treasured memories. Others are—well, let's just call them things you can't forget. While we all have our own lists of personal disasters, it's a pretty safe bet that somewhere on your list will be the first dent on your first car.

Few things in life are more brain-numbing than the first time you see a dent on pristine paint or a wrinkle on smooth metal. And if you think the shock of finding it was something, you were in for a real eye-opener when you went to get it repaired. You came face to face with the first Rule of Repair:

THINGS ALWAYS COST MORE THAN YOU THINK THEY DO

and sometimes more than you think they should.

Dings, dents, and rust are facts of life. No matter how well you care for your car, scrapes and bumps are unavoidable. They might not be your fault—you might not even be driving the car—but unless the only thing you do with your car is paint it gold and plant geraniums in it, its lifetime is going to be filled with trips to the automotive plastic surgeon.

It seems a bit magical to drop off an eyesore on Monday and have the damage disappear by Friday. Not only does the car look as good as new but it's often hard to see where the damage was in the first place. As a matter of fact, there's only one part of the whole process that makes it somewhat less than terrific, and that's paying for it.

Looking at the bottom line on a repair bill is often recommended by doctors as a good test of your cardiovascular system. Even the cost of repairing a simple dent can mean you'll be eating cold pizza for a week and a half. It might seem unfair; it might seem unreasonable; it might even seem unbelievable, but the high cost of body work is unavoidable simply because most of the final price comes from the cost of labor.

The better the repair, the more skilled the repairman. The more skilled the repairman, the more expensive his time. Accept it—that's just the way it is.

You might be overwhelmed by the array of hardware in a typical body shop, but you shouldn't be. The hammers and torches, compressors and grinders, drills and files are the smallest part of what it takes to eliminate the evidence of the time you zigged when you meant to zag. The real key to body work isn't spending money on tools, it's knowing how to use the stuff you buy. And you really need less stuff than you think.

I know you've heard this before, but here it is again: If you're willing to put in the time, you can do your own auto body repairs and save yourself a bundle of cash in the process. You don't have to add much to the collection of ordinary tools you have around the house to be able to handle the typical damage done by most fender benders. All you really need is a handful of tools, some basic skills, and—more important than anything else—the right attitude.

And so we arrive at the Golden Rule of Repair:

HOW HARD CAN IT BE

or, "I'm a smart guy and if he can do it, so can I." The simple fact that you're reading this is evidence that you're a smart guy and want to do your own repairs. (But we knew that all along.)

Doing your own body work means you set your own standards—repairs can be as good as you want them to be. The quality of the final job is only limited by the amount of time you're willing to spend and the amount of skill you have. I can't do anything about your time, but I can do a lot about your skill. If you're willing, so am I. By the time you work your way to the end of this book, you'll know how to do basic body repair, and you'll have a good time reading about it as well. Trust me.

As if that isn't enough, you'll become really good at estimating the amount of time a repair will take. Believe me, this is important because, even if you don't want to tackle a particular job yourself, you'll have a good idea of how much time the job should take. In addition, because time is the key ingredient in a body repair bill, you'll know when a ride to the garage will result in a trip to the cleaners.

1
CHAPTER

Getting Started

IF YOU ALREADY HAVE SOME EXPERIENCE DOING BODY REPAIR, YOU WON'T NEED to read this chapter. All we're going to do is talk about the basics—things like tools and safety, and some personal memories that have to do with the first time I tried doing some of the things covered in the next few chapters.

There's no reason in the world you can't all do the work described in this book. None of it requires that you be born with a special gift. Doing body work is not the same as becoming a concert violinist or a world-class soccer player. I'm the first to admit that not everyone has the ability to be great at this stuff. A part of it is like sculpturing, and some people are better than others at creating shapes. But unless you have your mind set on the complete restoration of a boat-tailed Cord, you can rest assured you have the ability to fix dents, scratches, and so on.

As we go through the steps involved in doing body repair, it should soon become obvious to you that everything we're doing is the result of a common-sense approach to the problem. You might not be familiar with the materials or the tools, but the logic behind the whole process is easy to understand.

If this is the first time you're trying your hand at body repair, you'll find the steps easy to follow, clearly described, and completely illustrated with photographs. Even though there are special tools used to make a repair go a lot faster, very few of them are absolutely necessary. Unless you're looking at the result of a major accident, you can do most repair work with common household tools and a large supply of elbow grease.

While there's nothing stopping you from spending the bucks for an air compressor, a grinder, a featheredger, and other tools, I wouldn't do it unless you're sure you want to do your own body work. It's a much better idea at first to make a small investment in materials and try a simple repair. If you enjoy it, terrific. If you don't, you've avoided some unnecessary expense.

Before we actually get started, let's spend a bit of time covering some of the fundamental equipment, materials, and procedures.

SAFETY

Safety comes first—always. Most of the rules you should follow while working on your car are more than likely things you would have done anyway. Safety is, if you think about it, just an exercise of common-sense judgment and an understanding of the tools and material you are using. But don't think that you should only be aware of the things we are talking about now. Safety procedures are not written in stone. There is no such thing as an exhaustive list of them because a lot of it depends on your work area, and that depends on the space you have available for working.

Even if you only use a modest amount of power tools, keep in mind that they can do a lot of damage to you. No matter what kind of repair you'll be doing, it's inevitable that you'll be producing good amounts of dust. Because of this, you should be wearing a respirator or breathing mask, common items sold in just about every hardware store. If you can't find them, ask the people in the store that supplies the materials you need to do the repair.

And don't forget that you'll be kicking up a lot more than dust as you work on the car. Larger particles of paint, body filler, and other materials will be flying through the air as well. Because you should be closely watching what you're doing while you're doing it, you've got to protect your eyes. The only way to do that is to get in the habit of wearing safety glasses while you work. Don't be fooled into thinking you can see better without them. If you don't wear them, you might not be able to see at all.

A good portion of the work you'll be doing involves the use of chemicals. While some of them are fairly harmless, even the most benign should be treated with respect. Compounds such as body filler and glazing putty are designed to stick to the surface of a car and, as a result, can stick to your skin as well. Although none of these chemicals is caustic, they can be murder to get off your hands when they're dry.

I can tell you from personal experience that it's just about impossible to get body filler (Bondo) onto a car without also getting it all over your hands at the same time. You can wear safety gloves while you're working, but I've always found it hard to do the job while I was wearing them. If you feel comfortable with them, wear them. If you don't, try to keep your hands as clean as possible and then make the job of getting the stuff off your hands your first priority as soon as you finish putting it on the car. Wet a rag with paint thinner and use that to clean the Bondo off your hands. As long as the body filler hasn't had a chance to harden completely, the paint thinner will make it soft enough to wipe off without taking any major chunks of skin along with it.

Most of the liquids you'll be using—primer, paint, etc.—are made with dryers that are particularly nasty. They all have a very sharp smell and, from the point of view of safety, there's one important rule you should commit to memory:

> ## IF IT SMELLS BAD, IT IS BAD

And while you might not be aware that it's doing any harm at the time you use it, you can never be sure it won't cause problems later on—especially if you get enough of it up your nose.

It should be perfectly obvious that you should only do body work in a well-ventilated area, but what that actually means might not be all that clear. It's not enough to keep a window or door open while you work on the car. That's no guarantee that the area is properly ventilated. A work area is well ventilated if there's enough of an air flow to get the fumes away from where you are working. You have to be sure the air is moving, that the fume-laden air is being replaced by fresh air, in order to protect yourself. If there's enough of a breeze with just an open door, that's fine, but you'll have to use fans if the air isn't moving at all. Be sure to set the fans on exhaust. Blowing air into the work area can tend both to trap the fumes inside and to blow in unwanted outside dust as well.

Don't rely totally on the movement of air to protect your lungs from the fumes. You need more protection than that. Anyone who uses paint or primer without putting on a breathing mask is just looking for trouble. Such masks only cost a few bucks, and they can save you from a lot of heavy medical bills. They might feel uncomfortable at first, but take a look at the dirt and discoloration that collects on them after you've been working for a while. Remember that all that stuff would have been inside you if it weren't for the mask.

You should do any kind of sanding or grinding with safety gloves on your hands. The dust you produce might seem innocuous enough, but the sparks that appear when you're grinding metal can do an impressive amount of damage to your skin. Protective gloves and clothing are easy ways to avoid a potential injury.

As you have probably discovered by now, the proper attitude toward safety is nothing more than an exercise in common sense. One thing that is often overlooked, however, is noise. The electric or air tools you use might not seem very loud, but remember that you'll be using them for extended periods of time and your head is going to be close to them while you're using them. Excessive and extended noise can affect your hearing and the fact that don't notice it at the time is only an indication that the damage is gradual and becomes more severe over time. Hearing loss begins with a lowered response to high frequencies, but it comes on so gradually that it's easy to miss. Any time you're working with power tools, you should wear plugs in your ears. There are several brands of disposable plugs that are both effective and easy to find. Most pharmacies carry them, and they're well worth the investment.

There's no absolute way to avoid accidents but you will minimize your chances of having them if you keep your work area well lighted. General lighting is a must, but it's a good idea to use local lighting to properly illuminate your work area. If you can't see what you're doing, not only are you increasing the risks of having an accident, but you're also minimizing the chances of doing the job properly.

If you want to be as safe as possible, there are lots of things to keep in mind when you're doing body work, or any other work. Make sure all your electrical outlets and tools are properly grounded, and be certain that all extension cords are designed to handle the current you'll be drawing through them. Keep all the electrical stuff away from water, and watch out for pools and puddles that happen to form on the floor.

Don't forget to keep a fully charged and operational fire extinguisher around the work area. A bucket of sand is a good idea, too.

There's no end to the list of safety precautions you can take to minimize the possibility of accidents. Most are easy to remember and some should be written down and nailed to the wall. Above all else, the most important rule to keep in mind is simply to:

> **THINK ABOUT STUFF BEFOREHAND**

because a lapse of memory can have serious consequences.

TOOLS

Body work can be an expensive proposition if you want to get things done in a hurry. The tools designed specifically for the job usually are aimed at the professional market, and that means they're going to have a fairly hefty price tag. But not all of them are really needed to get the job done. Some tools can make the job easier, faster, and a good deal more efficient, but that doesn't mean that you can't do anything without them.

The majority of work you'll go through when you're doing body repair involves sanding, grinding, and polishing. Each of these three activities is done with a dedicated tool when the work is done professionally in a shop. If you think about it, though, all these tools do is spin a disk around. It might be heavy and slow for a polisher, or faster and lighter for a sander, but you can do all these jobs with a good-quality electric drill and a good assortment of the right accessories. It might take longer than using the specialized tools but it's still better, faster, and a lot less tiring than sanding and polishing by hand. In addition, the fine sanding you have to do before painting can be done just as well with a standard orbital sander.

The one job that's difficult, if not impossible, to do without the right equipment is getting the paint on the car. Although there are lots of ways to get the paint from the can to the fender, the only way that works well is spraying. Some electric sprayers are designed for house painting, but none of these work well with auto paint. House paints like latex are lighter and can be handled by the centrifugal action of the electric paint sprayers. Auto paint is much heavier and the pigments are too thick for anything other than compressed-air sprayers. Fortunately, you can probably find a place near you that rents both the compressor and the spray gun.

Most of the non-power hand tools used in body repair are exactly the same as the ones you probably have around the house. A completely equipped body shop will have a bewildering array of hammers but, when you get right down to it, a hammer is a hammer is a hammer. The same can be said of vise grips, screwdrivers, and all the other hand tools you have around the house.

Just about the only hand tools you'll have to buy are dent pullers, squeegees, and cheese graters because nothing else can do their particular jobs. The function of a dent puller is obvious, and it's something you're going to have to buy. Almost every auto supply store carries these things and, since you probably won't need to buy more than one in a lifetime, it's a good idea to avoid buying either the cheapest or the most expensive. A medium-priced, moderately heavy-duty dent puller will be fine for most repairs—certainly for the kinds of repairs you should pick for your first attempt at body work.

Squeegees are needed to apply the Bondo and glazing putty to the car, and they're also used when you wet-sand the surface. They are made of plastic or rubber and, because they only cost a dollar or so, it's a good idea to keep several of them on hand.

A cheese grater is like a file, and it is used to do the rough shaping of the Bondo when it's put on the car. Its name comes from the fact that it works and looks just like a cheese grater. Cheese graters are made of a thin, springy metal and are fairly inexpensive. They also break easily, so you should have several of these around, too. The broken ones can be used for corners and other places where you have to file down the Bondo but don't have the room to maneuver.

MATERIALS

As we go through the various stages in repairing body damage, you're going to need several basic supplies. Don't rush out and buy everything at once because the supplies you'll need depend on the type of repair you're doing.

The most fundamental materials are those that are used in every type of repair—such things as Bondo, glazing putty, and primer. You should have an adequate supply of these when you start working on the car. Each brand has its own advantages and disadvantages but, when you get right down to it, all of them are good for most of the general type of repairs. Buy the brands that are most conveniently available and reasonably priced.

However, be a bit more careful when you buy primer. Some primers are only suitable for some kinds of paints. Check with the people in the store to make sure the primer you're going to buy is compatible with the type of paint you want to use. A mismatch of primer and paint will cause problems that might not show up until well after the repair is completely finished. No matter how terrific you feel when you finally complete the job, you'll feel equally awful a few months later if the paint starts cracking or peeling because it didn't adhere to the primer. Once again—just a matter of common sense.

The details involved in using all the materials and compounds are described at the appropriate stage of the repair job. However, don't take the words on these pages as a substitute for the ones written on the tubes and cans you buy at the store. Don't forget that there are a lot of companies making these supplies and that means there's a lot of competition among them. Manufacturers spend considerable money developing their products. They put instructions on the can to make it clear how their product should be used. Read the instructions carefully and follow all the directions given for mixing, preparing, applying, and finishing. Nobody knows as much about the product as the people who make it. Another useful piece of information you'll find on the container is the name of the solvents and thinners you can use with the product. Knowing how to clean up is just as important (and often more of a pain in the neck) as doing the job.

A FEW PERSONAL NOTES

The first time I ever had body work done on a car, I had no idea of what was involved. To me the bodyshop was a black box. I brought the car in wrinkled, and it came out straight. But the more I thought about it, the more I became amazed that it was possible to do something like that. Fold up a piece of aluminum foil and then try making it smooth again. It's not easy.

When you begin trying your hand at body work, you're going to find out that what seems easy in theory is really very tricky. It's no big deal to identify dents when they're a half-inch deep, but trying to figure out how to correct an irregularity that rises and falls only 1/8 inch or so over a distance of 3 or 4 inches is a different thing altogether. Running the palm of your hand over the surface will tell you that something's wrong, but knowing where you should bang or pull the metal to make everything smooth is not as easy. It's all a matter of practice and experience.

The secret to a successful repair is careful attention to detail and the ability to keep your objectives in mind. You have no idea how many hours can be eaten up when you're working to smooth off the body of a car. First you see the large dents and spend lots of time fixing them, all the while thinking that's all you want to do. As soon as they're smoothed out, however, you see smaller ones and are tempted to fix those as well. This sort of thing can go on forever because no matter how much time you put in, nothing is ever perfectly smooth.

The more time you put into metal repair, the better your repairs will be. When you become familiar with the materials you'll be using, the quality of your work will increase and the amount of time it takes to finish it will decrease. But these are the mechanical parts of the repair and, no matter how good you become, you have to be sure to judge the state of the repair with a healthy dose of common sense. Don't start anything without first having a good understanding of what you want to accomplish. And keep those goals uppermost in your mind as you do the work. Take it from me; it's easy to get sidetracked and wind up spending hours and hours fixing the slight irregularities that never bothered you before. Always keep the job in perspective.

One of the trickiest parts of body repair is covering the work area with Bondo. The first time I did it I got into trouble because it seemed to be a lot like plastering—something I knew how to do. This is a trap because, even though it seems similar, it's really not the same thing at all. If you poke a hole in a plaster wall, the only damage that's done is right at the point of impact; the rest of the wall doesn't change. When the metal on your car is dented, the damage extends well beyond the point of impact. The impact causes ripples to radiate out from the point of impact and, even though you might not notice them, they're there.

Fig. 1-1 By building up a series of progressively finer layers of different materials, an invisible repair can be made.

When you're making a plaster repair, the idea is to fill the hole with plaster and bring the level even with the wall immediately around the damage. When you're finished, the only place you should have new plaster is in the hole. When you're doing a metal repair, the Bondo fills the hole but is extended around the hole as well. The entire area, both the dent and the section around it, remains covered with Bondo. This is done to build a smooth surface over both the immediate damage and the slight deformities caused by the ripples. Before the repair was made, the damaged metal had many rises and falls. But after you sand the Bondo, you'll have a single, gradual rise that is completely unnoticeable.

The biggest mistake people make when they use Bondo for the first time is to sand away too much of it. When you start cutting down the Bondo, the goal is to leave a very thin skin of Bondo over the entire work area. Do not just fill in the dents. If you sand the Bondo down to the point where it's only filling the dents, you'll feel all sorts of irregularities when you run your hand over the work area. When you leave a thin skin on the surface, however, the entire area will feel perfectly uniform. And if you feather the edges where the Bondo meets the metal so the transition from one material to the other is very gradual, you'll have the foundation of a completely invisible repair.

Each stage of a repair is covered in detail later on in the book, but a good rule to follow is to define the work area as a bit too big rather than a bit too small. It's hard to clearly identify the extent of the damage because irregularities beyond the immediate damage aren't easy to spot. If you make it a rule to extend the Bondo 4 or 5 inches beyond the obvious damage you'll be increasing your chances of winding up with a successful, invisible repair.

It takes time to develop the skills needed to do a repair. In the beginning when everything is new, you'll undoubtedly waste as much time and material as I did. The first time I mixed up a batch of Bondo, I used too much hardener and the applicator got stuck on the body of the car. I had to cut it off, sand the surface clean, and start all over again. Fortunately, mistakes like this—even though absolutely everyone makes them—are the kind you only make once. Not only that, but there's really no way to avoid making them.

There's really no limit to the kinds of mistakes you can make when you're doing a repair. But if you work carefully and pay attention to what you're doing, you'll realize what you did wrong and what you have to do to correct it. Be positive. Mistakes aren't disasters; they're just things you have to correct and lessons you have to learn.

If you take your time and follow the steps in each chapter of this book, there's no reason you can't produce professional results. It might take you a bit longer than it would a professional, but you'll have the satisfaction of knowing that you did it yourself.

2
CHAPTER

Starting the Repair

BY THE TIME YOU'VE GOTTEN THIS FAR, YOU SHOULD REALIZE THAT THERE'S A world of difference between reading about body work and actually doing it yourself. Even someone with a black belt in cleverness is going to screw up the first time they try their hand at repairing a dent, so don't feel that you have to get everything perfect when you get started. There's no way that's going to happen. But don't worry about it, because no mistake you can possibly make will look worse than the damage you're trying to repair.

Now that we're going to get our hands dirty, we'll go through each step of the repair in detail and let you know what kind of materials you'll need along the way as you begin doing cosmetic surgery on your car.

There are special tools designed specifically for body work, but a lot of them just make things go faster and there's no reason you can't do the repair without them. It might take longer to do a particular job without them but, at this point, saving time is a luxury, not a necessity.

You can substitute ordinary household tools for some of the ones you see hanging on the wall in the store. Your common sense is the best guide in deciding whether or not you can substitute something you own for something you have to buy.

But the time has come, as someone once said, to get into it. A couple of things before we start working. I've said this before, and I'll probably say it again, but remember that safety counts for a lot. It won't get you anywhere on a bus, but if you're not careful, you might not be able to get on a bus in the first place. So, at the risk of boring everyone to death, here's the way things should be before you even look at a repair job.

1. Keep the work area well lighted. Mood lighting's terrific for wine and whimsy, not for work.

9

2. Have good ventilation. There's no doubt that some of the stuff you'll be using smells funny, but there's nothing at all funny about what it can do to you.
3. Protect your eyes. One small speck can do a lot of damage and if you don't believe that, why do you think the lenses on safety glasses are so full of scratches?
4. Wear a breathing mask. Since Bondo sticks so well to cars, imagine what it does to your lungs.

I could fill lots of lines with safety provisos and there would still be lots of things unlisted. It's impossible to mention everything. When you come right down to it, there's really only one thing you have to keep in mind and that's the Golden Rule of Repair:

DON'T FORGET TO THINK

If you remember this, everything else will fall into place. You're starting out with 10 fingers, and it would be a real plus to finish the job the same way.

SIZING UP THE JOB

No kidding, looking's what you have to do first. If you've ever taken a car to a body shop for repair, try to remember the first thing the guy did when you got there. That's right—all he did was kneel down next to the damage and look at it. You might have thought that was pretty silly because a dent is a dent is a dent. But I think you get the general idea.

Things aren't always what they seem to be, and that's true at the body shop as well. Taking a close look at the dent wasn't, as you might have thought, an indication that the guy needed glasses. He wasn't just looking at the damage you could see; he was looking for all the damage you couldn't see. There's a lot more to the car body than just the outer skin of metal, and it's always possible that these underparts are twisted or damaged as well.

If the impact that caused the dent also bent the metal under the skin, the job is going to be bigger than you thought at first. If there is unseen damage, limiting your repair to only the surface dent is kind of like putting makeup on measles—it might make things look better, but it's not solving the problem.

When you examine the damage, you're actually making several basic decisions about the route you're going to take in making the repair. The most elementary decision is whether the job is worth doing in the first place. It's not worth the bank's money to spend 25 cents to send you a letter saying you have 23 cents in savings. Auto body damage has to be weighed in the same way, regardless of how hard it is to take that point of view.

I'm the first to admit that cars can be a lot more than a simple possession. I've had the same car for more than 20 years, and my wife accuses me of giving it more attention than I give her. This might or might not be the case, but it is true that as far as I'm concerned, any damage to my car, is going to be repaired. I'd no more think of junking it than I would of junking my wife.

But back to the matter at hand. There are several things to keep in mind when you're assessing the damage. You have to weigh the amount of work needed to repair the car and decide if it's going to take more than elbow grease to get the job done. Remember, there's a point at which it becomes less expensive to replace a piece of metal rather than to repair it.

All this presupposes that you can see the complete extent of the damage, and that isn't always an easy thing to do. A lot of modern cars use very thin metal on body parts and depend on an underlying series of struts and baffles to strengthen them. This makes it easy to be misled when you're assessing the damage. An insignificant dent on a door could be hiding much more serious damage to the structural elements inside the door, and the only way you can know that is either to look inside the door, (a pain in the neck), or to have enough experience to recognize the problem.

Because it's always better to be safe than sorry, whenever you have a doubt about how deep the damage goes, spend the extra time to get a peek behind the metal and be sure you understand the amount of work involved in making the repair. If you fix the outer skin but leave the underlying structure a mess, you'll pay a price for it later because you'll probably have to do the job all over again. This is a good thing to avoid. Few things in life are as bad as having to do the same job twice.

PREPARING THE CAR

Because this is the first job we're going through together, we might as well be reasonable and keep it simple by tackling a simple dent. The only complication we'll add is that it's located someplace on the car where it's impossible to get to the back of the metal. Let's also assume that the underlying structure of the fender is still sound, and the only damage is the cosmetic stuff on the outer skin. If you were also faced with making repairs to strengthen the inner fender supports, this, of course, would be the time to do them. Cosmetic repairs are the last thing that get done but, as we'll see, a lot of the skills used for surface repairs are the same as the ones used under the surface.

A good example of this type of dent is one on the front of the fender just forward of the tire. Obviously, there's no way to get a hammer behind it. This is usually the case with modern cars because the back side of fenders and doors are honeycombed with support pieces. As a matter of fact, even if you attack the fender with wrenches and expose the back side, chances are that you won't have much access to the back side of the outer skin, anyway. What this means in terms of making the repair is that because the dent can't be hammered out, all

Fig. 2-1   The damaged fender can only be repaired from the outside. There's no easy way to get access behind the metal.

the work will have to be done from the outside. Traditionally, the tools used for banging out dents were the hammer and the dolly. But modern car construction, or the lack of it, has changed that to the hammer and the dent puller.

Because the first step in repairing a dent is to assess the damage, you need to have free access to the entire area. First, get rid of all the chrome and rubber trim around the dent. If the trim is damaged so much that it will be replaced anyway, you can be as cavalier as you want in taking it off the car—anything short of high explosives that manages to get the job done. However, if you want to be able to re-use the trim, you'll have to be a bit more careful. Trim can be held on with screws, bolts, clips, or glue and each has to be removed differently.

Most modern trim is held on with plastic clips and, unless you know something I don't, the clips are going to break as soon as you try to take the trim off. Use a screwdriver or some other thin piece of metal to lift up an edge of the trim so you can see where the clips are. If you're lucky enough to be able to squeeze them and pull them out of the holes in the body, you're ahead of the game. But don't be surprised if they snap as soon as you try to pull them off the body.

If the trim is glued to the body, the success you'll have getting it off depends entirely on the kind of glue that was used. You might be able to

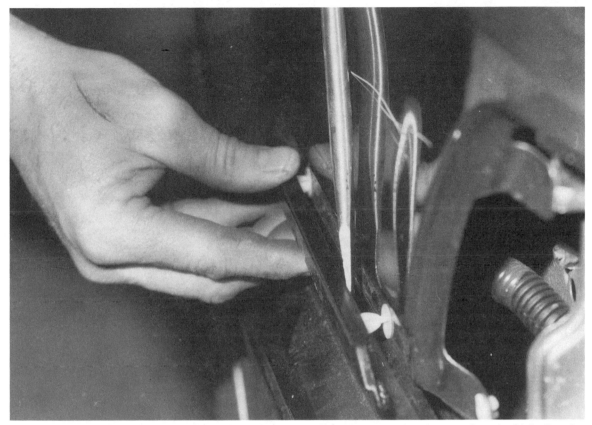

Fig. 2-2 Modern body trim is often attached with clips. Use a screwdriver to pry the trim away from the body. If you're lucky, the clips won't break.

increase your chances of getting the trim off by using a hair dryer to heat the glue. Get the trim and surrounding metal as hot as you can and try to get under a corner of the trim with a knife or screwdriver. If you manage to get that far, hold the corner up and aim the hot air right at the glue. As the glue heats up, you should be able to slowly pull the trim off the car. Remember that the object of this exercise is to save the trim, so don't worry about what might be happening to the body of the car. Any scratches or globs of glue that wind up on the body will be taken care of later, when you start the actual process of repairing the dent.

There might still be some car manufacturers that bolt the trim to the body but I haven't seen any lately. This is usually found on older cars. How easy it is to remove bolted-on trim depends on how easy it is to get behind the panel. Getting inside a trunk or hood is a piece of cake—they're made with that in mind. But getting to the inside of a door or fender can be murder—they were designed to be put together, not taken apart.

Fig. 2-3   Unbroken trim clips can be reused, but broken ones have to be replaced with new ones.

Remember that trim is usually easy to replace and it often makes more sense to sacrifice the old trim and replace it with new trim when the body repair is finished. You'll be saving a wad of cash by doing your own repair anyway, so the cost of new trim shouldn't mean all that much. Besides, new trim is a lot cleaner and shinier.

STRAIGHTENING THE METAL

Before you can attack the dent, you have to know exactly how big it is. The apparent damage isn't always the total damage because the depth of the dent decreases from the point of impact. It's hard to see slight deformities in the metal in the best circumstances and it can be harder in this case because the paint is usually undamaged. The only way to be sure you've found the full extent of the damage is to use both a metal straightedge and the palm of your hand to find it.

Run the palm of your hand across the dent. Start well before the damaged area to make sure you get a good feel for the undamaged metal. You'll be surprised to find out that touch is much more accurate than sight in measuring damage. You can feel changes in the metal much more accurately than you can

Fig. 2-4   The reflection of the straightedge makes it easier to judge the extent of the damage.

see them. This will be especially true later, when you've sanded away the paint and can't see a reflection in the surface.

Take a metal ruler and hold it against the fender. This will make it easy to see where the damage actually begins. If the surface has a gentle curve to it, bend the ruler against the surface so it follows the curve of the fender. Watch the reflection of the ruler in the paint because the distortion of the image will show you exactly where the damage is. The outer edges of the damage will still be hard to spot because the metal is much straighter there and, as a result, the ruler's reflection will be less distorted.

By using a combination of these two methods, (the metal straightedge and your palm), you'll be able to find the full extent of the damage. As soon as you've located it, take a pen and draw the outline of the dent on the fender. If you take a good look at the dent, you'll see that the metal has buckled in and out, forming creases and wrinkles that radiate out from the deepest point—the point of impact. Not only that, but the dent has really formed a crater on the

Fig. 2-5   Use a pen to mark the dent. Draw a circle to define the damaged area. Mark the center with an "X" and draw lines to mark the creases in the metal.

surface of the fender. The periphery of the dent is higher than the undamaged metal, and then the metal slopes down to the point of impact.

This might seem strange, but you can see it for yourself by carefully examining the damage. When the fender got hit, the metal actually stretched as it was being pushed in. Even if it were possible to push the metal flat, you would find that there's excess metal as a result of the impact. You can get the same effect by poking your finger into a piece of paper or cloth. The rim of the depression will be higher than the original surface.

It's important to understand this because the stretched metal of the dent will be thinner than the undamaged metal, so you have to be careful when you're pulling the dent out. Because there isn't as much thickness there, it's easy to grind and file your way through the metal entirely. The bottom line here is that the deeper the dent, the more care you should exercise in straightening it.

Take the pen and draw lines, following the major creases of the dent, from the point of impact to the edge of the damaged area. These lines are the ones you'll use to pull out the metal. Ideally, you want to pull the metal flat along the same lines created by the damage in the first place. Obviously it's not possible to pull along the entire length of each crease, but you can use the creases as a guide.

Fig. 2-6 Drill holes for the dent puller along the crease lines you've drawn in the dent.

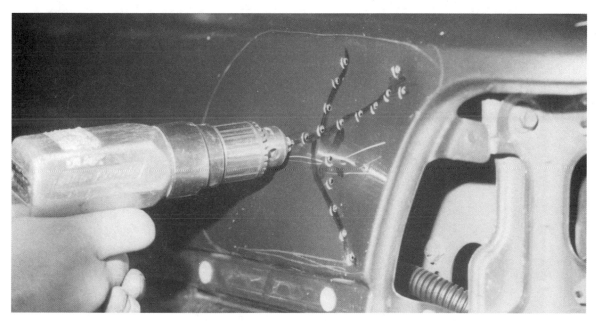

Fig. 2-7 Keep the holes at least a half inch apart, but never leave more than an inch and a half between them.

Next, drill holes for the dent puller along the crease lines you've drawn on the metal. The holes should be no less than a half inch apart. You can increase the spacing to an inch and a half if the damage covers a large area and the slope to the point of impact is fairly gentle. In general, the smaller and deeper the dent, the closer together you should drill the holes. The size of the holes should be slightly smaller than the thread on the end of the puller. Remember that the puller has to be able to grip the metal in order to pull out the dents. Make the holes too big and they'll be useless. Make them too small and you won't be able to thread in the puller. Use a piece of scrap metal to experiment with drill sizes. It's easy to make mistakes here, so a bit of practice is definitely worth the time.

Most dent pullers work well with eighth-inch holes but most dent-pulling operations use up a lot of eighth-inch bits—you break a lot of bits when you start holes in sheet metal. One good way to keep down the number of broken bits is—believe it or not—to break one intentionally. Break the bit off so that only a quarter-inch of the bit is left above the shaft. When you're using the bit to go through the sheet metal, you only need a quarter-inch of bit to peek out of the chuck. It takes a lot of pressure to go through the metal of the car, and hav-

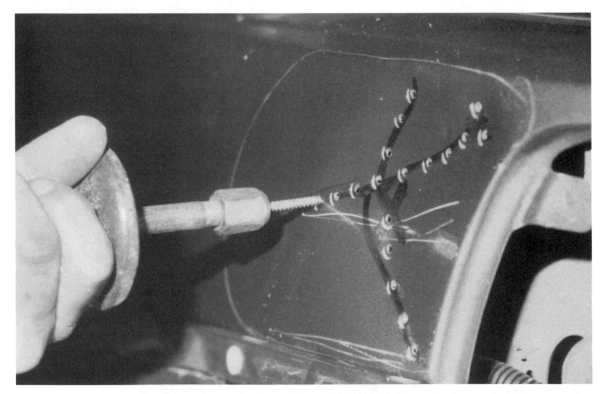

Fig. 2-8   Start using the dent puller on the holes at the periphery of the dent. You want to pull out the metal from the outer edges first and work your way to the center.

ing a long bit sticking out of the drill is almost a guarantee of snapping the bit. By keeping the bit nice and short, you can bear down with the drill and not have to worry about the bit suddenly snapping off and slamming your fingers into the fender. You won't lose your temper either—also a good thing.

When you start pulling out dents, you want to start with the holes at the periphery and work your way toward the middle. By doing it in the reverse order in which the dent was created, you'll be putting a minimum amount of stress on the metal. Don't worry about the raised part of the dent around the lip; we'll take care of that later. Your immediate job is to pull out the dent with a minimum amount of damage to the metal. By starting at the outside and working toward the middle, you will make the metal move as little as possible.

Remember that the dent is the shallowest at the periphery, so you only have to pull it out enough to make it flush with the rest of the fender. The idea here is to pull the dent out gradually because every time you pull one of the holes even, the metal toward the center is pulled out a bit as well. Work your way around in a spiral from the outside to the inside and, by the time you get to the center, the metal at the point of impact will be nearly flush to the surface of the fender.

When you pull out a dent, the idea is to make it get progressively smaller, and that's why you should pull from the outside to the center. If you pull from the center out, you'll not only wind up with more stretched metal but it will also

Fig. 2-9   The metal near the center of the dent will be moved by pulling the holes at the edges. When you work to the center, you'll find that the holes will only have to be pulled out slightly.

Fig. 2-10   If you've pulled a hole too far, use a hammer to gently bang the metal back down.

be hard to tell if the metal has been pulled until it's even with the surface of the fender. Raising the center while the periphery is still depressed creates a donut-shaped dent, puts even more tension on the metal, and makes it more difficult to tell when you should stop pulling.

As you work your way around the dent, keep feeling the surface to check the height. Don't try and get things perfectly even with the puller. You have to leave a bit of a depression for the Bondo you'll use later.

Words can't describe the amount of force you should use with the puller. If you pull too hard, you'll either ruin the hole or pull the metal out so far you'll have to hammer it back down later. If you pull too lightly, you won't get anywhere. Both of these are good things to avoid, and the only way to do that is to use the right amount of strength on the puller. Now, "right amount" is a less-than-useful term, but it's the only one that applies. All I can tell you is that if you don't have any idea what it means, learn by practicing on a piece of scrap metal. It might take some time, but you don't want to do your learning on the right front fender of your pride and joy. Trust me on this one. You really don't want to do that.

There are some things you should keep in mind as you're pulling out the dent. Make sure you're thinking of them as you spiral your way to the center of the damage.

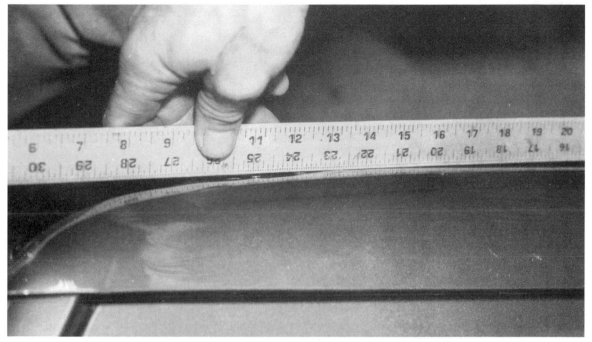

Fig. 2-11 The straightedge is the best way to check your work. You can see that the metal here is too high around the 22-inch mark of the ruler.

Fig. 2-12 Use the dent puller to hold the nearby metal as you bang down high spots with the hammer.

Remember that you don't want to pull the damaged area exactly even with the original surface of the fender. Leave the dent with a slight depression so there's room for a thin coat of Bondo. Even if you were able to use the puller to get the damaged surface perfectly even with the rest of the fender, you'd still have the holes you made to get the job done. Not only that, but the damaged metal gets really stressed, both as a result the original damage and the banging you have to do to repair it. The Bondo fills the holes and, when it's applied properly, actually adds a good deal of strength to the repair.

Unless you're the world's greatest something-or-other, you can't avoid pulling some of the holes out too far. Always keep a hammer handy to bang the high spots down. As you're straightening the metal with the puller, keep running your hand over the area. Just as you did when you were marking the damage, start with your hand on the undamaged metal and run it across the work area. If you have any doubts at all about how much you've pulled, use the straightedge to check it. Chances are the paint has been so marked up that you won't be able to tell anything from the reflection of the straightedge, but that's no problem because the edge of the ruler and the palm of your hand are perfectly adequate. If you find a high spot, hold the metal out with the puller and use the hammer to bang the metal down to the appropriate level.

You might find that you missed part of the dent when you originally marked it out. That's no big deal. All it means is that you'll have to drill some more holes and pull them out as well. A bit more time and a bit more work, but that's life.

CHECKING THE SHAPE

It's important to get the metal correctly shaped with the puller and the hammer because this part of the total job is when you do the most moving of the metal. As you do rest of the repair, you'll concentrate more on the finish and less on the shape. The amount of stuff you'll be doing directly to the metal will also decrease.

With that in mind, you should be very particular about giving your official okie-dokie to this part of the job. If you don't get it right at this stage of the game, correcting it is going to cause you a real load of brain damage later on, and we all know that one of the most important rules when you're doing anything is:

AVOID BRAIN DAMAGE

Fig. 2-13   Bend the metal straightedge to check the work you've done on curved surfaces.

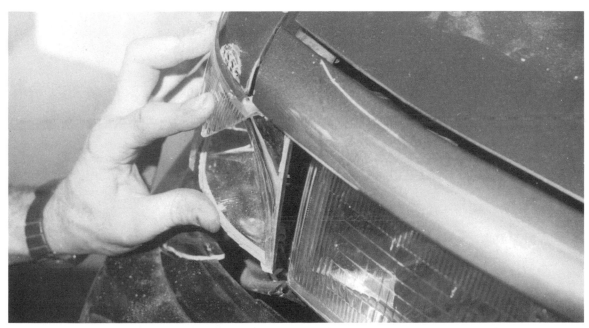

Fig. 2-14   Always check the body shape by refitting the lights and trim you removed when you started.

Fig. 2-15   If the paint is still intact, you can also use the reflection of the straightedge to check the extent of the repair. Compare this to Fig. 2-4.

you've been working. Slight changes in the position of the metal can make a big difference in the amount of work you'll have to do as we move along through the rest of the repair procedure. As you reshape the metal with the dent puller, you should frequently check on the alignment of the surface. If you've removed any lights, chrome, or body trim, hold them back on the car to check the progress of your repair. Use the straightedge, too, because it will show you any high or low spots that still need some work.

This is the one time when you should avoid using your hands to see how smooth you've made the surface. The burrs from the holes you've drilled are sharp, and if you rub your hands over the surface to check the contour, you're going to get cuts—Guaranteed.

You're not looking for perfection at this stage of the game because there's a lot more to do. The idea is to return the damaged area to a good approximation of the original shape. It's important to make sure that the edges of the dent fit in with the undamaged area and there are no high or low spots left in the work area.

If you find any places that you're not happy with, take the time to get them the way you want them. Remember that very few surfaces on a car are perfectly straight. Most have at least one curve or, more often, several curves to the surface—usually in several directions as well.

Keep running your hand over the area and using the straightedge to check your work. Again, you're not trying for an absolutely smooth surface; you're only concerned with the general shape of the metal. The former will come later, and the latter is what makes the former possible in the first place.

The final word—and the most important one—at this point of the repair is:

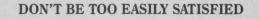

DON'T BE TOO EASILY SATISFIED

A shrug of your shoulders here will cause a slap in the head later on, and a lot of extra work.

CLEANING THE WORK SURFACE

Now that the dent has been pulled out and the damaged area has been shaped to fit the original curve of the fender, you have to clean the whole surface off to prepare it for the Bondo.

Use a rough, open-grit paper to remove the paint from the area you've just straightened. The best way to get rid of the paint is to use a grinder, but you can

Fig. 2-16 Start grinding away the paint at the edges of the repair. Use a coarse paper, and be sure to keep the grinder moving.

do it with a moderately high-speed drill as well. It might take a bit longer with a drill, but there's no point in spending unnecessary money; it's better off in your pocket.

Keep going over the work area until you've removed all the paint because Bondo adheres better to bare metal. Start at the center of the dent, work your way to the outside, and go a few inches into the undamaged area. The reason for removing paint in the good area around the dent is to give you space to blend the Bondo into the curve.

Use a light touch with the grinder. The point of this whole exercise is to remove paint, not metal. You wouldn't believe how thin the metal is on some cars, and you certainly don't want to find that out accidentally while you're doing a repair on your own car. You can always patch it up, but it's a colossal waste of time. Not a mistake you want to make, especially on your own car.

Keep the grinder moving all the time. If you want to stop for a minute, lift it off the surface and turn it off. Not paying attention to what you're doing can result in holes—but at least you can see those and fix them later. Moving the grinder too slowly or holding it completely still can overheat the metal and cause it to warp out of shape. This is really bad because you might not notice it until much later. Having to remove lots of Bondo—and paint as well if you don't spot the problem until you've reached that stage—can ruin your whole day.

Fig. 2-17   Work the grinder slowly across the entire area using a light pressure on the metal.

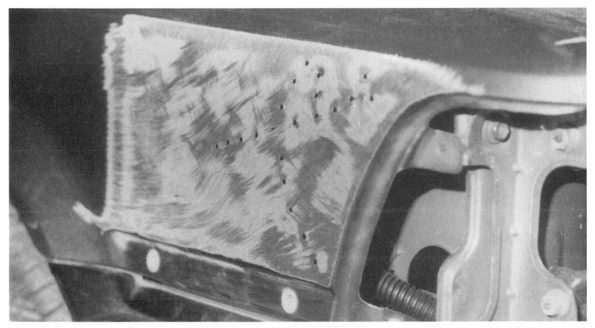

Fig. 2-18   All the paint should be removed by the grinder.

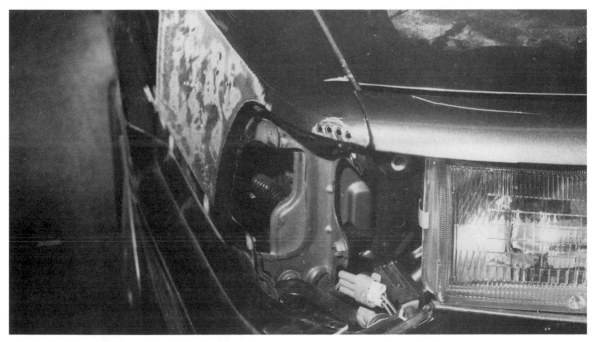

Fig. 2-19   The small area at the front of the fender was missed earlier, and holes were drilled to pull it out.

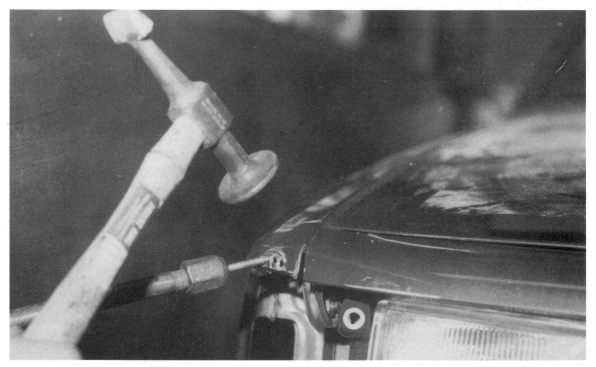

Fig. 2-20   Small areas, like the front of the fender, should be pulled out gently because the shape of the metal is more important here than on large areas.

Fig. 2-21   Because there's no easy reference for a straightedge, you can check the shape of the fender front visually by seeing how it aligns with nearby undamaged metal.

Fig. 2-22   Be careful when grinding away the paint on small areas. The metal can easily be damaged, and the edges can be burnt by the grinder.

Fig. 2-23   When grinding near the edge, always have the grinder turning toward the edge. Grinding into the edge can chew away the edges of the metal.

Grinding away the paint is a pretty straightforward operation, and you shouldn't run into any major problems as long as you watch what you're doing and remember to keep the grinder moving around the work area. Just don't forget that the grinder is removing metal as well as paint. The main reason for doing body work in the first place is to replace the paint, but it's a real drag to have to replace metal. Don't just think before you grind, try to think while you're grinding as well.

It may have seemed to take a long time and a lot of work to get to this point, but you're now ready to begin making the repair invisible. From now on, you'll shift your concern from the metal itself to the contour of the car. Because it's impossible to restore the original shape of the fender by beating and pulling on the metal, the final restoration has to be done with Bondo.

That doesn't mean that you can put away the tools you were using to work directly on the metal. Most of the contouring you'll be doing from here on will be with a special file called a cheese grater, which is designed to be used with Bondo, several different grades of sandpaper, and a lot of elbow grease. However, you might still find it necessary to bang down a few spots that you might have overlooked. Hey, nobody's perfect.

Check the work you've done up to this point to make sure the metal is free of paint. Once you start covering things up with Bondo and primer, you won't be able to see anything you've overlooked, and it might turn out that the only way you'll know you made a mistake is when the paint starts to crack months later. You really don't want that to happen. Really.

3
CHAPTER

Restoring the Contour

ONCE UPON A TIME, RESTORING THE CONTOUR WAS DONE WITH LEAD. THOSE DAYS are gone. Some people will tell you how much better repairs are when they're done with lead and, to a certain extent, they're absolutely right. But only to a certain extent.

Melting lead onto a surface to fill out the repair has several advantages, but there are disadvantages as well. There's no argument that lead bonds better to the metal of the car, but you have to be very careful about preparing the surface. It has to be completely free of paint and dust, and you should wash it down with a mild acid before you start melting the lead onto the metal. Having to melt the lead with a torch as you're applying it to the repair is also a pain in the neck and takes a lot more time as well. In addition, you can't cover the whole surface at once. With lead, it's always a little bit at a time.

Before leaving the subject of lead forever let me just mention that if you're thinking of using it, don't forget that it's lead. A lot has been learned since lead was in common use, and one of the things you should keep in mind is that lead is apparently not as inert as people once believed. Lead fumes are dangerous. It was with good reason that it stopped being used as a catalyst in gasoline. Lead isn't as bad as mercury, but it's bad enough.

There are several varieties of body filler on the market and most of the companies that make it have their own name for it. There are many marketing claims for each product, but they're all more alike than different. Bondo, or whatever product you buy, will come as a two-part mix. The larger container is the actual plastic compound and the other, usually a small tube, is the hardener. The two have to be mixed together before they can be used, and the mixing proportions should be included in the package. Follow the instructions carefully because a batch of improperly mixed Bondo is time and money down the drain.

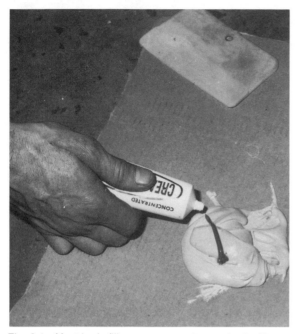

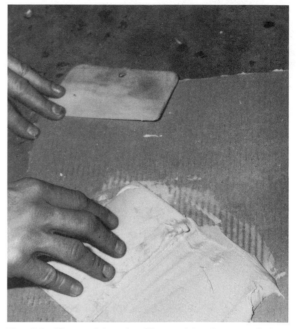

Fig. 3-1 Most body fillers come as a two-part mix. Use a two-inch strip of hardener for each golf-ball size lump of filler. Mix them on a clean surface.

Fig. 3-2 Keep mixing the filler and hardener until they reach a uniform consistency and color. Use pressure to get rid of air bubbles as you mix.

The mix of chemicals makes the Bondo harden, much the same as it does with two-part epoxy glue, and using the wrong proportions when you mix the Bondo will have the same results. A shortage of hardener means the body filler will take a long time to harden and it might ultimately peel off the car. Use too much hardener and the material will turn hard before you have a chance to put it on the car. Each brand has its own particular characteristics but if you're not sure exactly how to mix it, a good rule of thumb is to use a 2-inch strip of hardener for a golf-ball-sized lump of Bondo.

Do your mixing on a clean surface, and make sure the two compounds are thoroughly mixed. The Bondo and the hardener are usually two different colors, so keep mixing them until the color is uniform. Don't stir them together; keep folding the Bondo into itself. The action is more like kneading dough than beating an egg. A stirring action causes air bubbles to form, and they'll be a pain in the neck to deal with later.

APPLYING THE BONDO

Once the Bondo is ready, use a rubber or plastic applicator to put it on the car. You can usually buy applicators at the same place you got the Bondo. The goal in

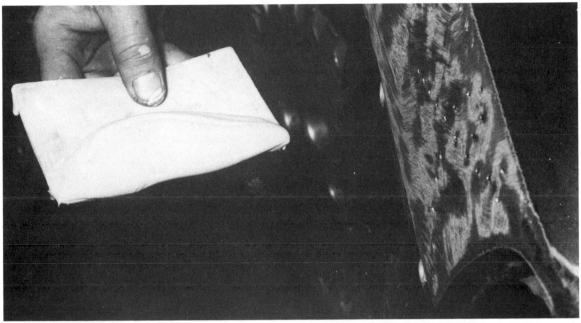

Fig. 3-3   Use a plastic applicator to apply the Bondo to the car. Put the Bondo on the edge of the applicator to allow you to control how the Bondo is applied to the metal.

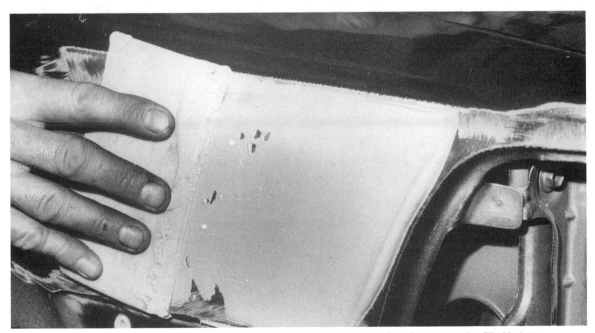

Fig. 3-4   Spread a smooth, thin coat of Bondo on the metal. Any air holes or missed areas can be filled in later.

applying the Bondo is to wind up with a coat of compound that's about an $1/8 - 1/4$ inch thick, and the best way to achieve this result is to put it on a strip at a time. The process is similar to plastering, but when you're working with Bondo, you don't have to worry about getting it perfectly smooth; you'll be cutting it down with the cheese grater as soon as it gets hard.

If you make the coat too thick, you'll have to do more work to cut it down later. If you get the coat of Bondo too thin, there won't be enough on the area to shape into the contour of the metal. Work smoothly and steadily. Don't worry if the Bondo drips or runs because you'll have the time and opportunity to take care of those things later. The first few strips of Bondo you put on the car will probably be messy, but it shouldn't take too much practice to get the hang of it. Remember, you'll always be able to fix your mistakes later, so the worst that can happen is that you'll have to do a bit of extra work.

As soon as you finish applying the Bondo, clean the applicator and the work area. If you wait, the Bondo will get hard and the clean-up will probably be more work than repairing the fender—the kind of mistake you only make once.

Fig. 3-5   Don't worry about having Bondo over the edge of the metal. The excess can be sanded later.

Fig. 3-6 Cover the work area completely with Bondo and let it harden. The excess Bondo can be removed during sanding.

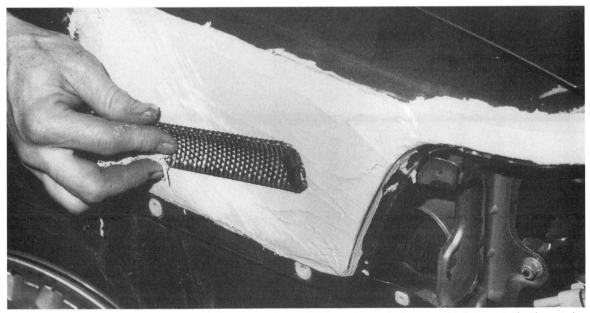

Fig. 3-7 Work the cheese grater diagonally across the Bondo. Horizontal or vertical cuts tend to leave ruts that have to be filled in with more Bondo.

Fig. 3-8   You should use the cheese grater to cut the Bondo to a rough approximation of the shape of the metal. The fine shaping will be done with the second coat of Bondo.

Next, cut the Bondo with a cheese grater. This is a straightforward process, but it takes a bit of experience to know when to do it. You want to get started before the Bondo has completely cured. If you wait too long, the Bondo will be too hard for the cheese grater. If the Bondo is too soft, cutting it with the cheese grater will pull it off the metal because there won't be enough adhesion yet between the Bondo and the metal. Don't cut the Bondo until it feels hard to the touch but still has a bit of give to it when you apply pressure. Once you become more familiar with Bondo, you'll be able to pick the exact moment to start cutting it down with the cheese grater. But at the beginning, just don't let the Bondo get too hard. You can start cutting it down when it feels like a hard gel.

When you're working with the cheese grater, remember that you're not trying to get a perfect surface. The cheese grater is a fairly crude tool, and all you want to do is get the excess Bondo off the car. The idea is to match the contour of the fender, not make the surface perfectly smooth.

Use a fairly light pressure with the cheese grater to keep from gouging deep grooves in the Bondo. Start at one of the upper corners of the work surface and move the cheese grater diagonally across the covered area. If you cut in a straight horizontal or vertical direction, you're running the risk of cutting ripples into the area because it's hard to maintain exactly the same amount of

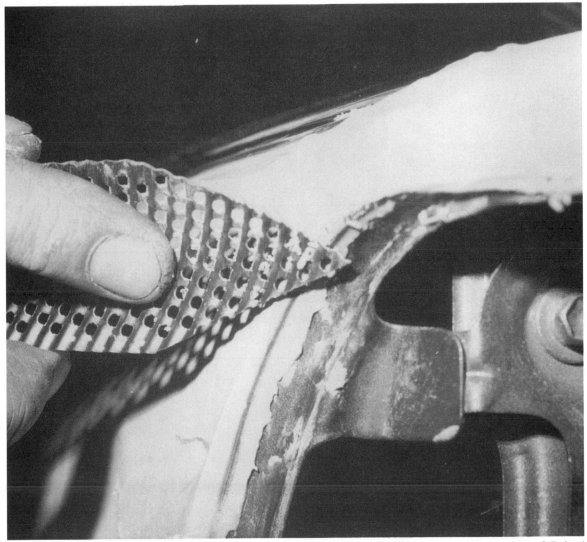

Fig. 3-9　Cut one cheese grater to a point to allow you to work the Bondo in areas too small and too curved for a full-sized cheese grater.

pressure as you go around the work area. Start your cuts with the cheese grater over the good metal just outside the work area to give you a feel for the shape of the fender and to make it easier for you to judge the amount of Bondo you want to remove.

Chances are pretty good that either the Bondo coating the metal is thicker in some spots than others, or the metal underneath the Bondo is uneven. More than likely, both will be true. If metal starts to show through in spots before

Fig. 3-10 If high spots of metal show through the Bondo, hammer them down and cover them with more Bondo.

Fig. 3-11 Check the small areas carefully. If the metal shows through the Bondo or the dent puller holes appear, bang them down and cover them with more Bondo.

Fig. 3-12   The work with the cheese grater is done when the contour of the surface matches the final shape of the metal.

you've completely cut down the Bondo, take a hammer and carefully bang those areas down. Make a depression about an inch or so wider than the metal spot. You will have to mix up a bit more Bondo to cover the metal, and adding the extra space around the high spot is a bit of insurance that the metal surrounding the high spot won't show through.

You might find that air has been trapped in the Bondo as a result of your

Fig. 3-13   The scratches left by the cheese grater will be smoothed off later by sanding.

being somewhat less than careful when you were mixing it. When you find these spots, you'll have to fill them with more Bondo and give it time to harden to the point that you can start cutting it down. If you add more Bondo to the work surface, make sure you get rid of all the dust and loose Bondo particles that are sticking to the surface. If you forget to do this, you can affect the final strength of the repair and, sooner or later, moisture will get into the Bondo and cracks or other imperfections will show up after the repair is finished.

This is only the first cut of the first coat of Bondo, so you can be somewhat tolerant of the overall shape of the surface. You're only trying to get it to roughly match the final shape, so you should call the first cut finished when it's a bit too low, rather than try to take the surface down to exactly the same level as the original fender. The cheese grater leaves slight depressions in the Bondo so judge the level by keeping an eye on the low spots, not the high ones.

As with most things in this business, the only way to know when a job is finished is through experience. Until you get to that point, just remember to do too little rather than too much. In this case, run your hand over the work surface to estimate how close the surface is to the original shape of the metal. It's also a good idea to use a straightedge to be sure you aren't cutting gradual val-

Fig. 3-14   The first coat of Bondo should bring you very close to the final shape of the metal.

leys into the surface. Such shallow depressions are hard to feel with your hand or see on a rough surface. The only way you can spot them in time to fix them is to use the ruler frequently. It only takes a second to check, and it can save a lot of brain damage later on.

SANDING DOWN THE SURFACE

Once you've decided that you can put your official okie-dokie on the first cut with the cheese grater, it's time to sand it smooth. As with the first coat of

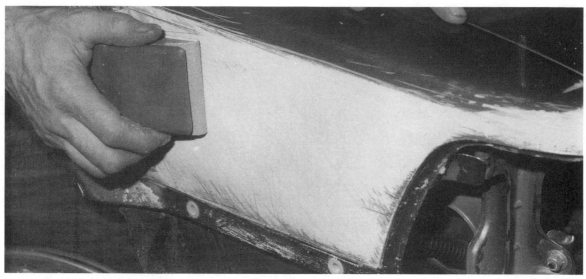

Fig. 3-15   Once the Bondo has been cut with the cheese grater, the marks left on the surface can be removed with sandpaper.

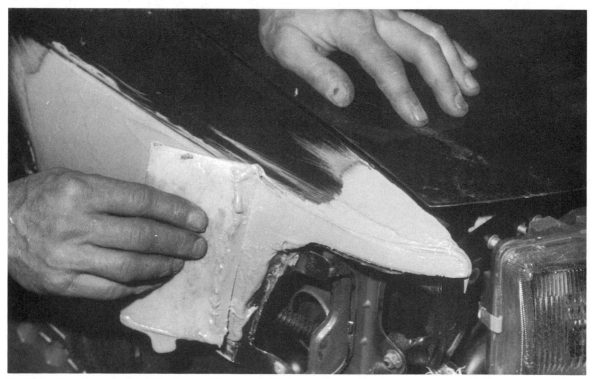

Fig. 3-16   The second coat of Bondo should be much thinner than the first one.

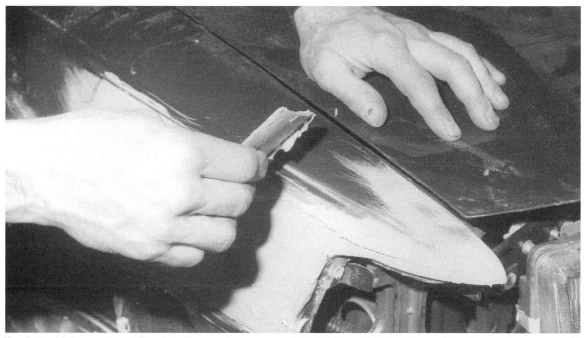

Fig. 3-17 Make sure to get Bondo in the small areas around the lights and trim. Neatness doesn't count because you'll clean things up by sanding the surface later.

Bondo, what you're after is a rough match to the contour of the fender, not a finished surface. The only goal you should have in mind as you start sanding is to smooth off the surface of the Bondo so you can see where you are and get an idea of how much Bondo to mix up for the second coat. Yes, you will have to do this again.

Put a piece of 40 grit paper in a sanding block. Start sanding at the top of the work surface and work your way down to the bottom. The paper is pretty rough, so don't bear down too heavily as you rub or you'll be getting rid of Bondo you want to keep. All you're trying to do is smooth off the surface.

The sanding block is good for the flat areas, but there are bound to be some small areas you'll want to do with the paper in your hand. No matter what kind of car you're working on or what part of the body you're trying to repair, there's always some corner or edge that you won't be able to do the easy way. I think it's a natural law of the universe, like gravity. Don't skimp on the sandpaper. Number 40 paper has a fairly open grit, but it does block up after a while. Change the paper whenever you find that the piece you're using is getting too smooth or taking too long to cut. Never work harder than you have to.

When you've finished sanding down the first coat of Bondo, you're ready to put on the second coat. Make sure the surface is clean and free of dust. It's easy to forget to do this but—take my word for it—you'll be reminded of it later.

Fig. 3-18   Cover the edges of the metal well. You may have to make allowances in the shape when you start refitting the lights and trim.

Fig. 3-19   The second coat of Bondo should extend beyond the first coat. Compare this photograph to the one on Figure 3-6.

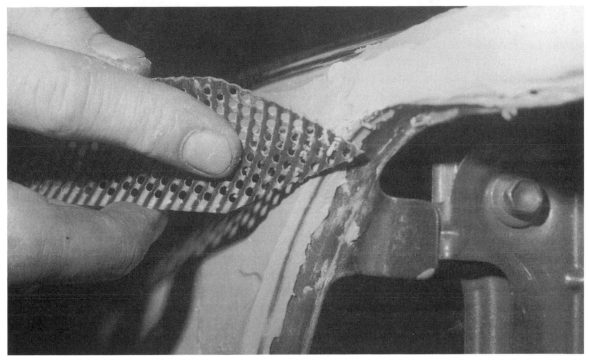

Fig. 3-20   The second coat of Bondo will need less cutting with the cheese grater than was needed by the first coat. Make sure to clean the small restricted areas around the trim and light locations.

Because this is the second and, yes, the final coat of Bondo, it doesn't have to be as thick as the first coat. The metal is already covered and you're applying it on a smooth surface, so you'll need a lot less Bondo for the job. Mix up about half as much as you did earlier and use more pressure with the applicator than you did when you applied the first coat. Heavier pressure will give you a thinner coat. Spread the second coat of Bondo out onto the surrounding metal areas using even more pressure. This will tend to thin out the Bondo at the edges of the work area and make it easier to blend, or feather, the surface of the repair into the surrounding metal area.

You'll finish the second coat of Bondo in much the same way as you did the first coat, with two exceptions: You'll be doing less work with the cheese grater—that's a good thing—and a lot more work with the sandpaper—that's just the way it is.

Be careful when cutting with the cheese grater. This will probably be the final coat of Bondo, and you have to pay close attention to both the height of the surface and the shape of the fender. All the material you'll be putting on top of the Bondo is designed to get the surface ready for painting. Bondo itself is intended to create the correct shape. If you don't get it here, it's gone.

Make a single pass over the surface with the cheese grater, and then check the contour with both your hand and the straightedge. If you have any doubts about how far to go, leave the surface a bit too high and take it down with the sandpaper. It might take longer to get the job done this way, but there's less of a chance you'll mess it up by going to far.

Just as you did with the first coat of Bondo, do the initial sanding with 40 grit paper. The purpose of using rough paper is only to remove the marks left by the cheese grater, so don't oversand any of the Bondo. As soon as marks are sanded off, move on to another part of the work area. Keep this up until all the marks are gone.

Don't forget to use a sanding block. Start at an upper corner of the repair and work down diagonally, checking the line of the surface as you go. Run your hand across the repair to make sure you're matching the contour correctly, and do frequent checks with the straightedge.

You might be tempted to sand the large areas without the sanding block, but that's not a good idea. Working with the sandpaper directly in your hand might give you the feeling that you have more control but—and trust me on this—that's just a feeling, not reality. You can sand a flat area correctly only if you hold the sandpaper flat against the work surface, and that means you should hold it in a sanding block, not in your hand. Unless you're either a martian or a mutant, it's impossible to have an equal amount of pressure across the surface of the sandpaper when you're using your fingers to apply pressure.

PREPARING THE SURFACE

Once the rough sanding is done, you're at the same point you were when you finished the first coat of Bondo. The difference now is that you're looking at the surface from the perspective of preparing it to be painted. If you look closely at the surface of the Bondo, you'll see that rough sandpaper leaves—no surprise—rough sanding scratches. No matter how smooth the surface feels to your hand, you better believe the scratches will show up when you put on the paint. Up to this point your only concern has been the shape of the fender. From now on, you should consider the texture of the surface.

After sanding with the rough paper, you should be able to see the shape of the final repair. The surface of the Bondo should be flush with the original surface, and you should see no depressions, bumps, lumps, or other irregularities. The shape should pass the now-famous straightedge test and, if you close your eyes and rub the palm of your hand across the repair, you should only feel a difference in texture, not height.

You are now ready to prepare the surface for painting. Each step from now on is aimed at getting rid of the scratches left by the previous step. The scratches on the surrounding metal and paint might look terrible, but they'll be cut down to a manageable size as you go to finer and finer sandpaper.

Before going any further, let's take a minute or so to discuss how the surface should be sanded. If you go to a body shop and watch someone making a repair like the one we're doing together, you'll see a lot of machinery used to sand down the surfaces. What you won't see is a lot of time spent in hand sanding. Remember that the guys in the body shop have a lot more experience, and the sanding machinery they're using is expensive—really expensive. If you have deep enough pockets, nothing is preventing you from going out and buying one of everything you see in the shop. All it takes is a trip to the store and a dent in your bankbook to have the world's best and most expensive equipment. No problem.

What you won't get at the store is the experience you need to know how to use these tools properly. Remember, tools that let you do a job quickly also have the power to mess up a job quickly. The difference is experience. Until you know what you're doing, it pays to be conservative and cautious. While it's true that hand sanding requires more time to get the job done, it's also true that fixing mistakes takes even longer. If you really want to use some machinery, there's good news in store for you: This is the point in the job where even a beginner can safely get some electrical help.

You're finished blasting away huge amounts of Bondo. From here on, your only concern is getting the surface ready for paint so at this point, you can substitute an orbital sander for the sanding block. As a matter of fact, an orbital sander will probably do a better job on flat areas because it tends to leave fewer sanding marks than hand sanding.

Any orbital sander will work well with the materials you'll be using on the car and, besides saving a lot of sweat, it will leave much finer scratches on the surface. You can do as good a job by hand, but it's going to take a lot more rubbing to get it done.

The bottom line here is that if you have an orbital sander, there's no reason you can't use it, no matter how inexperienced you are. If you've managed to get this far, you've got the skill to use the machine. If you don't have one, you might want to think about buying one. Doing this repair yourself is saving you a lot more than the cost of the machine, and anything that saves wear and tear on your muscles is always a good idea.

Whether you use an orbital sander or sand by hand, the basic steps are the same. The enemies you're after this time are the scratches you've put on the surface, so you'll need to sand with finer and finer grades of paper until you reach a point where the paper is so fine that the scratches it leaves can be hidden by the paint.

So far, the only paper you've been using is 40-grit. The next grade to use is 100-grit, this will get rid of the existing scratches and leave much finer ones on the surface. In case you're wondering why you can't just move directly to the final grade of paper you'll need in this stage of the repair, take a second to think about it. It's true that the finer the paper, the smoother the finish it leaves. But it's also true that the finer the paper, the less it cuts. If you go directly from rough to fine paper, you'll be able to get the job done but it's going to take a lot more work. Using several intermediate grades might use up more paper, but it also takes less time and a lot less work. One of the unwritten rules of life is:

DON'T OVERDO IT

It's always a good idea to follow the path of least resistance, so let's keep muscle strain to a minimum.

Using 100-grit paper, follow the same path across the repair you did with the 40-grit paper. Start at one of the upper corners and work your way diagonally down to the opposite corner. Keep brushing the dust off the surface as you sand so you can tell when the deep scratches have disappeared. The 100-grit paper will leave scratches of its own, but they won't be nearly as deep as the others.

Don't forget to use a sanding block. Even though the 100-grit paper takes less material off the surface, you can still sand in some serious ruts if you're not careful. If you work the sandpaper with your hand, the uneven finger pressure can easily put depressions in the Bondo and—believe it or not—this can be more of a problem with fine paper than with the rough paper you used earlier.

Because the rough paper cuts so quickly, unwanted ruts are fairly deep and can be easily felt by running your hand over the surface. A rut left by fine paper is much shallower and easy to miss when you examine the work. It's possible for your hand to slide right over any slight irregularities left by the sanding, but don't think for a minute that a rut you can't feel is something you can ignore. No matter what kind of body repair you plan to do now or in the future, you should never put this rule far out of your mind.

PAINT HIDES NOTHING

Even a small repair requires a lot of work to correct properly, and the temptation to keep muscle work to a minimum is always there. Resolve diminishes in direct proportion to the amount of sweat produced. This happens to everyone and you have to make sure that your determination remains constant throughout the job.

The only way to be absolutely certain that you're not sanding ruts into the surface is to use a straightedge. The palm of your hand is a good guide, but the straightedge is the definitive tool. You might not be able to see a small sanding depression; you might not feel it with your hand; it might even be just about unnoticeable with the straightedge. But don't think it's going to disappear. The minute you cover it with paint, the problem is going to be just as evident as looking in a fun-house mirror. Believe it.

With that warning in mind—and the knowledge that you'll be really unhappy if the final job suffers because you were less than careful—take the time to run the straightedge over the work surface every few minutes or so. With auto body repair, as with a lot of other things, the longer you wait to correct a problem, the more work you have to do to fix it. If you don't do five minutes of extra sanding now, you might not spot the problem until the car is finally painted—and it's a world-class understatement to say it will take more than five minutes to fix it then.

But back to work. Even though the scratches left by the 100-grit paper are finer than those left by the 40-grit, they're still too coarse for painting. Once you completely sand the surface, switch to 180 grit paper and go over the surface once again. This paper will leave marks fine enough to be hidden by the rest of the materials you'll be using as you get the repair ready for painting.

Keep checking your line with the straightedge to make sure you're maintaining the contour of the surface. Don't forget to include the metal surrounding the repair when you're sanding with the fine paper. The area you'll be painting will be larger than the damaged area alone. It will include the surrounding that you've been sanding and even some of the unmarked painted surface beyond that because it's impossible to have perfect control of the coverage when you spray paint. In addition, you want to be able to blend the new paint into the old paint to minimize the difference between the two. When we get into painting, you'll see that it's almost impossible to perfectly match the original color and new paint has a different finish than stuff that's been on the car for a number of years.

After sanding with the 180-grit paper, make a final test of the contour by temporarily putting the trim and other body parts back on the car. You're not putting them back permanently, just securely enough to be held in position so you can check the shape and fit of the repair. Chances are you'll have to do a bit more sanding to bring the surface contour into correct alignment. Try the finest sandpaper (180 grit) for these final adjustments because anything coarser is going to take the surface down too quickly and leave marks that will have to be sanded down even further.

If, when the parts are on the car, you find that some areas of the repair are too low—how does the old line go?—I've got some good news and some bad news. The bad news is that you're going to have mix more Bondo and build up the surface. The good news is that you probably won't need very much, and you're better off finding out about it now than later.

There's a fine line between good and good enough, and where it is depends on you. I'm pretty sure most of us would work to correct something 1/4 inch off—maybe even something 1/8 inch off. Anything less than that, as far as I'm concerned, is a finished job. But that's me.

If you're the kind of person who is bothered by an irregularity of less than 1/8 inch, feel free to get the surfaces as perfect as you like. After all, this is, America, and if you're one of those people who can't bring themselves to step on the cracks in the sidewalk, you've got the freedom to go for whatever you call perfection. Hey, it's your car, your time, and you're the one doing the sweating.

No one can tell you when this part of the job is finished. You're the one who has to define the end of the job because you're the one who has to be satisfied. The only guideline I can offer is that too good a repair can be as noticeable as one that's too bad. Check over the rest of the car and try to match your repair to the quality of other areas of the car. If you want to get it better than the original, you're running the risk of having your work lose the desirable goal of invisibility. Don't ever forget that the more successful your repair, the less you should be able to notice it.

APPLYING PRIMER AND GLAZING PUTTY

Everything you've done so far has been to restore the original shape of the metal. At this point, the Bondo is on the car, the surface has been sanded down with 180-grit paper, and there's a smooth transition between the Bondo and the metal at the edge of the repair (called feather-edging). Now it's time to prepare the surface for painting.

Before you can do anything more to the surface, you have to cover the Bondo to protect it from moisture and to create a surface that you can get per-

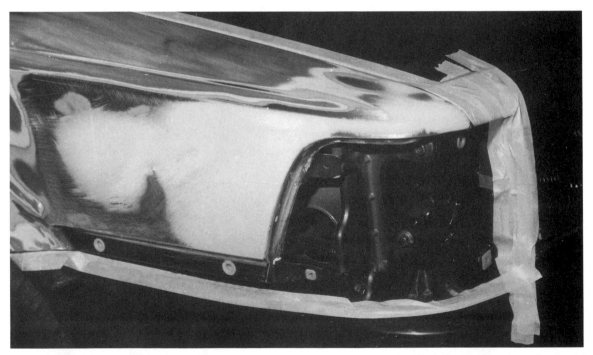

Fig. 3-21   Mark the edge of the area to be painted with masking tape. Follow the lines in the car body or the ends of metal panels whenever you can.

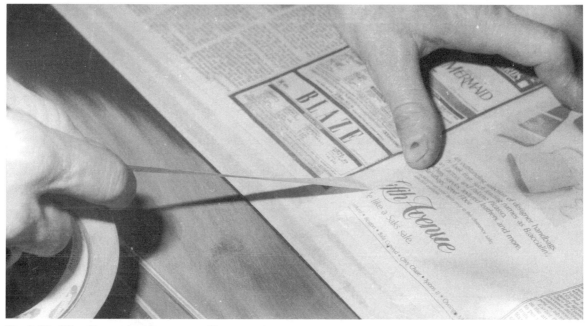

Fig. 3-22 Cover the surrounding areas with tape and newspaper to protect them from the overspray of primer.

Fig. 3-23 Be sure the surrounding areas are well covered. The primer, or any liquid you happen to be spraying, has a nasty habit of getting sprayed in areas you don't want to be sprayed.

fectly smooth. Even if you sand the Bondo with the world's finest paper, you'll never get a perfectly smooth surface because the material itself has an inherent grain that will always be evident, no matter how much work you do.

The best material to cover the Bondo is primer and, that's exactly what you'll be using now. Primer provides an adhesive surface for the top coat of glazing putty we'll be adding (more about that later on), and it seals the surface of the Bondo.

Before you can spray the primer on the repair, you have to mask off the surrounding area to protect it from accidental overspray. Use a roll of paper masking tape to mark off the circumference of the area you want to spray with primer. Give yourself a few inches beyond the area you worked with the sandpaper. This area includes both the Bondo and the surrounding metal you've scratched up.

Once the area is marked out, you can use newspaper to mask off the rest of the car. There's no need to protect more than about 2 feet outside the area

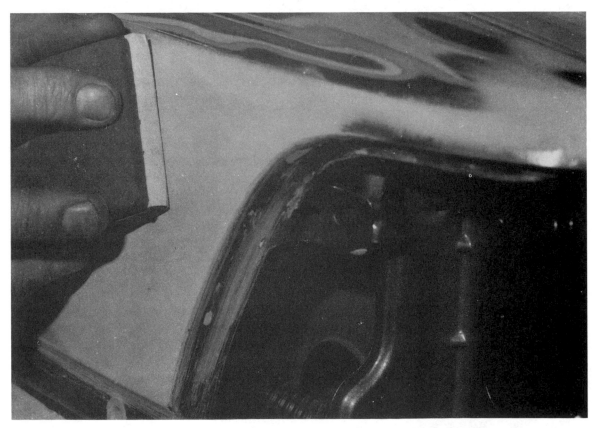

Fig. 3-24   Go over the surface carefully before you prime it. It has to be clean, and this is the last time you'll be able to see the Bondo and easily sand away any deep scratches.

you're going to spray. Getting the paper on the car is a pain in the neck, but you can make it a bit easier by putting the masking tape on the edge of the paper and then putting the taped paper on the car. Lay the paper on a flat surface and put the tape along the edge of the paper, leaving half the width of the tape over the edge so it will stick to the car.

Lay the paper on the car by putting the tape right on top of the tape you used to mark out the area to be sprayed. Primer is a liquid, so it's going to build up a bit at the tape line and the double thickness of tape will help prevent the primer from creeping under the paper. Once you have the work area masked off, make sure the paper is protecting the surface, watching out for bends or openings between the individual pieces of paper. Don't skimp with the tape. If you see a potential problem, nail it down with some extra tape. It's much easier to add tape than to remove primer.

Next spray the primer on the surface. This is a significant step because it not only marks the official end to a major part of the repair work, but it's also the first time you'll be able to completely judge the quality of the work. The primer might only be an undercoating but it's still a kind of paint. When you put it on the car, you'll be able to see exactly how well you finished off the Bondo. All the irregularities and imperfections that show up in the final paint show up

Fig. 3-25   Apply the primer in several thin coats rather than one heavy one. Keep the can moving all the time at a constant speed.

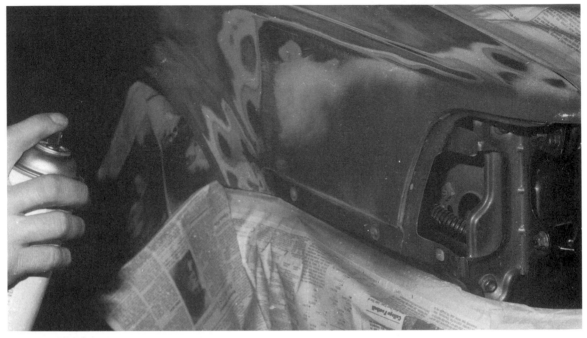

Fig. 3-26　Start spraying at the top and work your way in horizontal passes to the bottom of the work area.

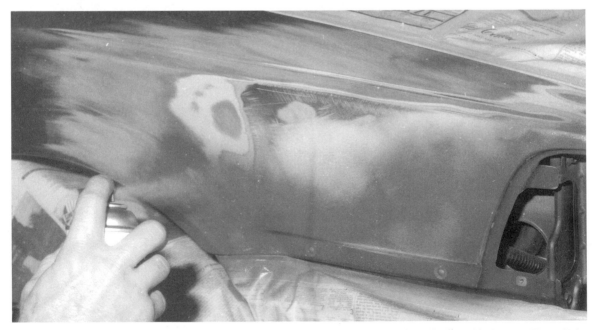

Fig. 3-27　Avoid the temptation to overspray any one particular area during a horizontal pass with the can. The rule for primer is better too little than too much.

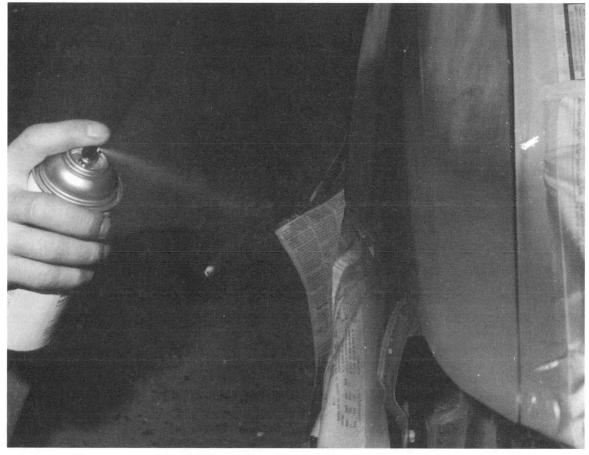

Fig. 3-28   Keep the can about a foot from the surface as you spray the primer on the car. Spraying too close or too far from the car will result in uneven coverage.

with the primer as well. You might need to do some touch up work with the Bondo and respray part of the work with primer. But let's not be pessimistic.

There are several brands of primer available, but they're all more alike than they are different. The choice of which one to use depends on what you can conveniently buy in a store. In any event, it's most convenient to get it in aerosol spray. Just about the only considerations you should have are the toxicity of the dryers in the primer and, if that's the way you are, how damaging the can's propellant is to the environment.

Before applying the primer, clean off the work surface. Any dust or other stuff you leave on will be trapped under the primer, and—as they say in the technical journals—that's not a good thing. The surface of the car isn't the only place you'll get dirt, so the nozzle of the can has to be clean, too. Even a new can of primer tends to spit a bit before the spray comes out evenly.

Keeping in mind both the need for adequate ventilation and the possibility that the primer spray is flammable, point the can away from the car and press the nozzle. As soon as you see that the can has stopped spitting and the spray is smooth and uniform, begin priming the car.

Move the can across the repair, starting at the top and working your way in horizontal passes to the bottom. Keep the can moving to avoid putting too much primer in any one area. The idea is to build up several thin coats, not to put on one thick coat. Thin coats don't run, and they dry better. Don't extend the spraying past the paper; change directions before you get there. If you build up a heavy coat of primer over the tape, you're going to have problems when you remove the tape from the car because the primer may lift off with the tape.

You can add successive coats of primer, one right after another, because the primer dries fairly quickly. When you reach the bottom of the repair, immediately go back to the top and start the next coat. As the primer begins covering the Bondo, you'll be able to see how well you did the repair. While the primer is wet, even a small irregularity will be evident in the reflection, and you're the one who has to decide if it has to be redone or if it can be ignored.

If you see something you want to fix, stop spraying and give the primer a chance to dry—usually about 10 or 15 minutes. Make the repair, and start spraying it again with primer.

How many passes you should make with the primer depends—as you can well imagine—on how slowly you move the can, how heavy the spray is, the particular brand, etc. As a general rule, if you keep the can about 12 inches from the surface and move at about a foot a second, you'll need about three or four light passes over the surface of the repair. The primer is fairly thick-bodied and adheres well to the Bondo, so it won't take long to apply it to the surface. The idea is to get a uniform color—it helps to use a primer with a different color than the Bondo—and uniform coverage. The instructions on the can will give you a more detailed idea of when you have enough primer on the surface. Just remember that you get a sufficient thickness by adding many thin coats, not a few thick ones.

You can fast-dry the primer with a hair dryer. However, the primer dries by itself in about 15 minutes, so the extra work isn't worth the minimal amount time it saves. A few clues you can use to tell when the primer is dry enough: The smell coming from the driers disappears, and the surface stops feeling tacky. If you want to be extra sure, spray a glob of Bondo as often as you spray the surface of the car and test the dryness of the glob.

Once the primer is dry, examine the work surface carefully for any irregularities that require touch-up. This is the best time to do it and, if you change your mind later, you'll have to do a lot more work to fix it. If you're happy with the appearance of the repair so far, you're ready to prepare the surface for painting.

The main idea behind all surface preparation once the metal has been straightened is to cover the repair with a series of materials that provide increasingly smoother surfaces. The final step and smoothest material is obviously the paint, but you have to add one more layer before you can start thinking about that.

Glazing putty, the last layer needed for the surface before the paint, is very much like the spackle used to repair plaster walls. When it dries, it has an extremely smooth surface and easily covers all the fine scratches left by the 180-grit paper. As you can tell by looking at your own repair, the primer dried into all the surface scratches. Then again, the primer is really just a particular variety of paint and, as I told you earlier (but you might not have believed until now):

PAINT HIDES NOTHING

So if the surface has scratches, the scratches will be seen.

Most glazing putties are single compounds, so you don't have to mix them before you use them. We're not going to be doing any heavy sanding on top of the putty, so you should apply it in a very thin coat. If you spread it evenly, you won't need more than one coat on the surface, but you might have to go over parts of the area a second or, at most, a third time to get it all covered.

Fig. 3-29   A thin, flexible rubber squeegee is the ideal tool for applying the glazing putty.

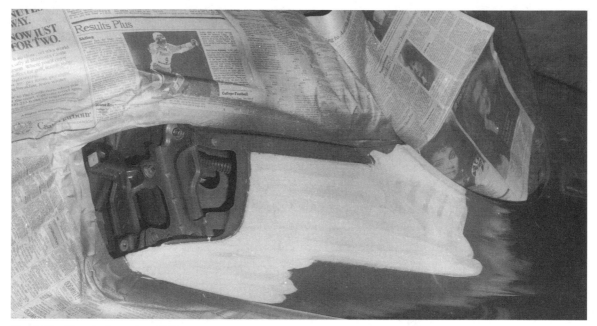

Fig. 3-30   The glazing putty will fill any scratches that are left on the surface of the repair.

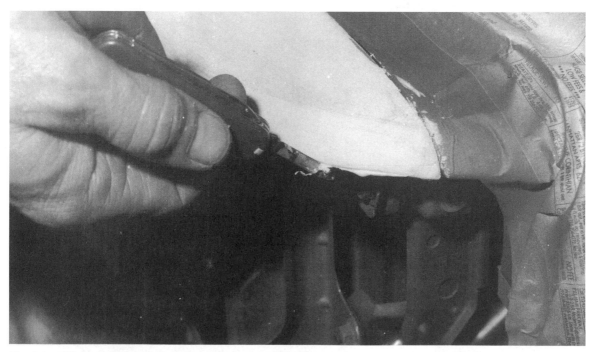

Fig. 3-31   When the putty dries, use a small knife or single-edged razor blade to trim away the excess at the edges.

Just as with spackle, the best way to apply the putty is to put a small amount at a time on the applicator and apply pressure to spread a thin coat on the surface. An ideal applicator is a thin rubber squeegee. It has enough body to spread a thin coat, but it is still flexible enough to fit around the curves and bends of the car's contour.

When you apply the putty, leave the paper you put on when you were getting ready to prime the surface. You want to overlap putty past the Bondo areas and over the scratched metal that surrounds them. Each material you put on the surface is going to spread further than the previous one. The idea is to build up progressively thinner layers from the center of the repair to the undamaged surface. When you do the final light sanding, these layers should provide perfectly smooth transition from the repair to the original surface. When you finally apply the paint, the border of the repair will disappear completely because the repair will be invisibly blended into the surface. At least that's what it says on page 12 of the manual.

Use a small knife to cut away any excess putty that might have gone over the edge of the surface. This happens in areas like the edge of a fender, or anywhere the metal takes a sharp turn. The putty dries very fast so don't spend too much time applying it to the surface. You'll find that you tend to get a buildup of dry putty on the rubber applicator. In order to spread the putty smoothly on the surface, make it a habit to keep the applicator—especially the working edge—as clean as possible. Stop work every so often to scrape off the dry putty. If you nick or cut the edge of the applicator, throw it away and use a new one. You can't apply a smooth coat of putty if you're using anything less than a smooth edge.

Once you have applied the putty, allow it to dry. The length of time it takes varies according to the brand, temperature, and so on, but you should be able to work on it after about 15 minutes (fast drying) to one hour (slow drying).

FINE SANDING

By now you have got an extremely smooth material on the surface of the repair, but there are still marks left from the rubber applicator. As you might have guessed, the only way to get rid of these marks is to sand them by hand. The difference between the sanding you've done previously and the kind of sanding you'll be doing from here on is that now the magic words are:

> **LESS IS BETTER**

Remember—the only things going on top of the putty are primer and paint.

Ever since Ben Hur's chariot race, there have been two schools of thought about final sanding—wet and dry.

Fig. 3-32   Light sanding with fine paper will get rid of the applicator marks.

Fig. 3-33   Use small pieces of fine paper to sand off excess putty and to create sharp edges and corners.

Fig. 3-34 A final coat of primer will make it easier to see whether there are any remaining scratches and will also prepare the surface for painting.

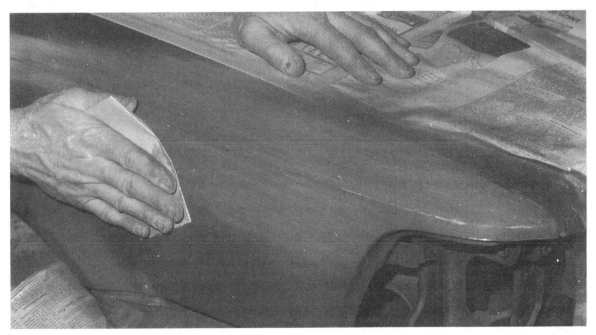

Fig. 3-35 Wet-sanding the final coat of primer creates a much smoother finish. Use 600, 1200, or even finer grit paper when you wet-sand the primer.

There's no argument that wet sanding is better because it gives you a smoother finish. The paper tends to fill with particles and, as you would expect, transfers a smoother surface to the car. But we all know that there's no such thing as a free lunch, and that's as true here as it is anywhere else. Wet sanding takes longer to do because it cuts less with each stroke of the paper.

A wet-sanded surface also tends to produce a finish much closer to the original factory finish found on most cars. The choice of which way to go is entirely up to you and, once again, the only guideline I can offer is that a body repair is supposed to be invisible. You can always spot something that's poorly done, and the same is true with a repair that produces a finish better than the rest of the car's finish.

Most body shops sand with dry paper because it's a lot faster and creates a perfectly good finish. Remember that wood is dry-sanded.

If you decide to wet-sand the surface, you'll need a rubber squeegee to periodically wipe away the water. Because the idea behind the final sanding is to remove scratches and smooth off the surface, you have to remove the water to see if there are any marks on the surface. The surface tension of the water will cause it to fill the scratches while you sand so you won't be able to judge your progress. Wet-sanding means sanding a bit, wiping a bit, and then looking a bit—over and over again.

A light touch with 180-grit paper will get rid of the marks left by the applicator. Pay particular attention to the edges of the work area; there's a good chance that you'll find a slight lip where the putty ends. Feel the work area with your hand to judge exactly how smooth the surface is. This is the only way you can tell how much work you've done and how much is left to do. Don't worry about very fine scratches that can't be easily sanded out. A lot of them won't show in the final repair and, if you make a mistake, you can always add a bit more putty to cover it up.

Remember that it's easier to sand stuff off than to put it on all over again. Be sparing with the paper, and keep it as free from dust as possible. If the paper starts to block up, hit it with a flat stick to beat out the dirt. Because you're doing very light sanding, you should be sure to use the sanding block rather than your hand. Finger pressure is uneven. This far into the repair, it would be a shame to inadvertently sand a rut into the surface and have to go all the way back to the Bondo to smooth it off again. Remember that you're only sanding away the applicator marks.

When the marks and scratches are gone, use tape and paper to mask off the work area again and apply a second coat of primer to the surface. You should spray this second coat just as you did the earlier one. You want to build up a series of successively smoother layers with fewer and finer scratches.

Once the second coat dries, examine it for any scratches that might be left and sand the whole surface, wet or dry, with 400-grit paper. It's not really necessary to wet-sand the primer because it has a lot of body and will tend to be very smooth right out of the can. The only way to judge the smoothness of the surface is with your hand and, now that you're at the last step, you should be running your palm across the surface as often as you do the paper.

Do the sanding with a block, rather than with your hand, especially on the large, flat areas of the repair. The paper is very fine and the touch is very light, so we're cutting the material on the surface very slowly and carefully.

Once you decide that everything is smooth and free of scratches, you can pat yourself on the back because the only thing left on the repair is actually painting the surface. "Only," however, is a relative word. When we get there, you'll see that matching, mixing, applying, and polishing the paint has its own special set of pitfalls to avoid and problems to solve.

4
CHAPTER

Repairing Rust
and Rot

No matter what sort of job you want or have to do to the body of your car, the more experience you get, the more you'll understand that most repair jobs are similar. The only difference between repairing a dent and curing a spot that's rusted away is the amount of work you'll have to do. That's not as silly as it sounds because when you actually do the rust repair, you'll go through the same steps, covered in the preceding chapter, for dealing with a simple dent. With the dent repair, you worked with existing metal. With rust or rot, you first have to replace the bad or missing metal before you can start taking care of the contour and finish.

There are two basic methods of healing a spot that's either rusted thin or rotted away completely, and which one you choose depends on the extent of the damage. You can't repair something that isn't there in the first place, so the most fundamental decision you have to make is how you want to go about replacing the missing metal. Although many materials can be used, the two standard choices are sheet metal or a special kind of Bondo.

Not long ago the only way to take care of rot was to make a metal replacement. This kind of repair is still the strongest and most permanent kind you can make. If you're looking at a really large patch of rust or rot—something like a completely diseased and mostly missing rocker panel—metal is the only way to go because you need structural strength as well as a new surface that can be finished to match the rest of the car.

Making new metal for a car always involves a lot of work, especially if you need to cover a large area. It also requires techniques and skills, such as various kinds of welding, that are well outside the scope of this book. Even adding small pieces of metal is a detailed business that takes more time, special tools, and a lot more work to do properly. Fortunately for all of us, some years ago the wonderful world of technology got interested in the auto body business and came up with a variety of fiberglass reinforced materials that can be used in place of metal.

These "super" versions of Bondo are very strong and, while they don't have the structural strength of metal, they're more than strong enough to be used in place of metal for a substantial number of repairs. A repair made like this won't be as durable or last as long as a metal repair but "last as long" is a relative term. Let's keep in mind that every repair has a certain lifetime for any repair, no matter what kind of material you use. This is even true of the original material the factory used on the car body—after all, the reason you're making this repair is because the car's original metal has vaporized.

The steps involved in repairing rust or rot spots are pretty much the same, regardless of whether you use metal or super Bondo. The only differences, have to do with the particular requirements of the material you decide to use for your repair.

Using metal adds a few steps to the job, so we'll go through the process of making a metal patch and getting it on the car body. Once this has been done, the rest of the procedure is identical to a repair made using only super Bondo.

CLEARING THE WORK SURFACE

As you should know by now, the first step in any body repair is to examine the damage and make a realistic assessment of the amount of work to be done. When you're dealing with rust or rot, it's usually hard to tell exactly how extensive the damage is without first cleaning the surface and getting rid of the surrounding paint. Bubbling on the paint or small dots of rust that show through the paint are indications that there's rot or rust hiding under the surface.

You won't know how much paint to clean off until you know how wide the damaged area is. On the other hand, you can't tell how wide the damage is until you remove the paint. The way to get around this somewhat paradoxical situation is to pick a place on the car near the center of the damage and use it as a starting point.

Just as when you were repairing a dent, you can't do anything to the surface until you've removed all the trim. You can try to save it if you want but since it is a rusted area, the trim probably isn't worth saving. There are, of course, exceptions to this rule. If the trim is made of plastic—such as lights or reflectors—and you can get it off the car in one piece, you might as well spend the extra time to remove it in one piece. The same is true if you know that it's harder to find a new piece than it is to safely remove the old piece, as was the case with my 20-year-old Jag. Once you have the trim removed, you're ready to begin dealing with the rust and rot.

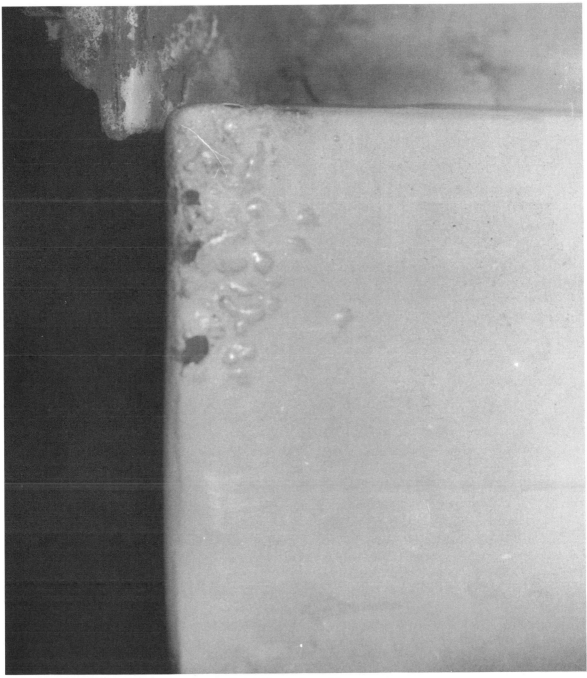

Fig. 4-1   The first sign of rusting metal is usually bubbling in the paint.

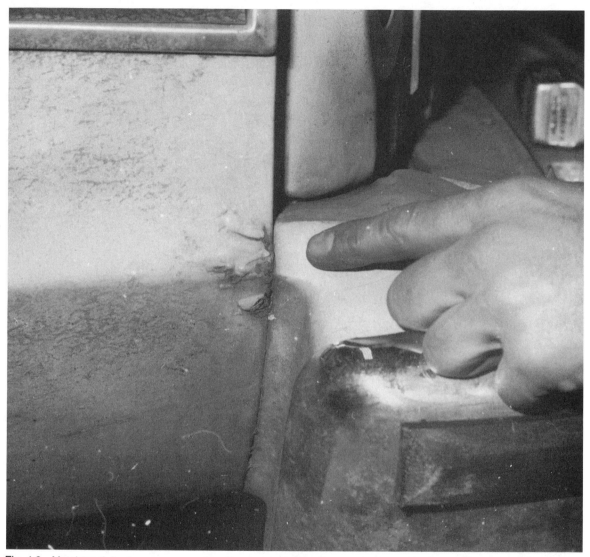

Fig. 4-2   Metal repair is also necessary when there are cracks and tears showing through the paint.

You can remove the paint by sanding, grinding, or using a chemical paint remover. However, just as in the last chapter, the best way to remove the paint is to grind it off. If you know at the outset that you are dealing with a large area, you can use paint remover. On the other hand, we have no idea how much rust is under the paint so it's better to bite the bullet and get out the grinder. You can also use a standard electric drill and a sanding attachment with coarse, open-grit sanding disks.

Fig. 4-3   Just as with any body repair, all the trim has to be removed before you start work.

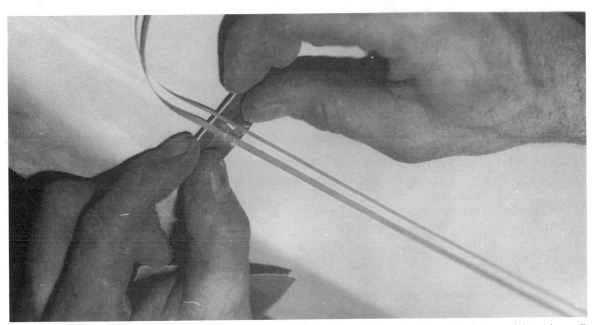

Fig. 4-4   Pinstripes are just decals that can easily be removed by using a single-edged razor blade to peel the stripes off the car.

Before you attack the surface, examine it carefully and make sure the rust hasn't created any sharp edges or points of metal. If you find any, bang them down with a hammer before you start sanding. Otherwise, the edges could get caught on the grinder and wreck the paper. Not only will you go through a lot of paper, but you'll also risk doing some serious damage to the backing pad on the grinder. If the rot has left sharp points and, even after you bang them down, you're worried that they still might get caught in the grinder, cut them down to size with a metal file.

Start at the point you've picked and widen the area by moving the grinder in constantly wider circles. Remember not to hold the grinder stationary on the metal because the friction generates a lot of heat. Remember heat can warp the metal. The grinder removes metal as well as it removes paint, so if you don't keep it constantly moving you might grind a hole in the surface. You don't want to grind through metal when repairing a simple dent, and you certainly don't want to now because the rust has undoubtedly thinned and weakened the metal. Car metal these days is nothing like the strong car metal of days gone by, so it pays to be extra careful when working with the grinder.

Fig. 4-5   Grind away the paint carefully, making sure the grinder is removing paint, not metal.

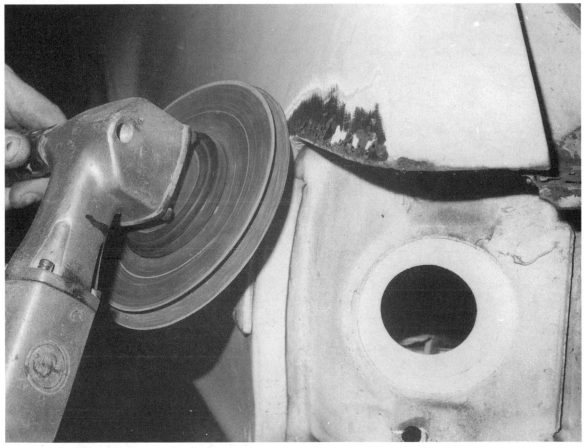

Fig. 4-6   Keep the grinder moving to avoid overheating the metal, and make sure the wheel turns from the body toward the edge of the metal. Grinding into the edge can damage the metal.

As you work your way down to the metal, you might be in for a few surprises. If you're not the original owner of the car, you can think of the paint removal process as an exercise in auto archeology; each layer you remove is a step backwards in the history of the car. Although you probably won't stumble across gold doubloons or ancient artifacts, you might see layers of ancient paint or Bondo. I always find it interesting to see what colors had been chosen for the car in the past. There's no accounting for taste.

Clean off the work area until you're satisfied that the surrounding area is good metal. Then take a minute to examine the work area. Pay particular attention to the edges of the metal in areas where the rot has eaten holes in the car body. You might find that the metal is so thin you can easily snap it off with your fingers. If that is the case, get rid of the really thin metal and use a file to blunt the sharp edges. Even though you'll be covering them up later, until you do,

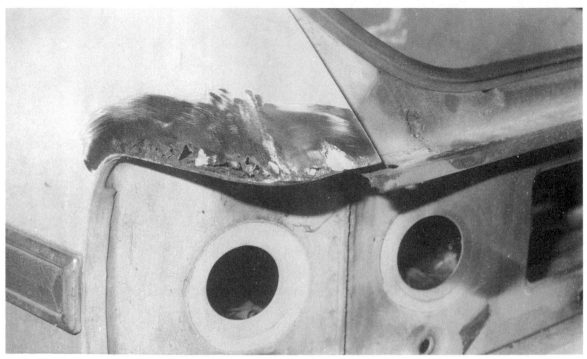

Fig. 4-7   Extend the work area beyond the rot by grinding the paint off some of the good metal surrounding the damage.

Fig. 4-8   Remove any material that's trapped behind the metal, file down the sharp edges, and get rid of metal that's so thin it can be snapped off with your fingers.

sharp edges are only accidents waiting to happen. And they will happen—trust me on this.

Exercise a bit of common sense in disposing of metal you think is too thin. You have to make a judgment; weigh the amount of thin metal you're removing against the amount of metal left in the damaged area. Don't remove too much metal, no matter how thin it is. You run the risk of losing the shape of the body. Remember that the metal was put there for both aesthetic and structural reasons. It's all well and good to properly prepare the work surface, but if all you

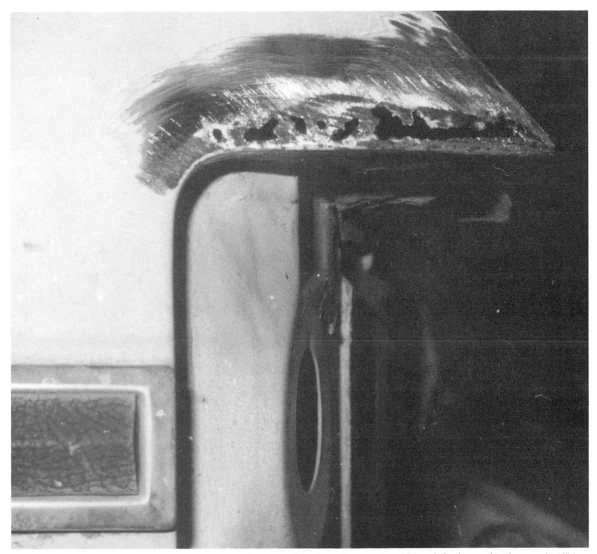

Fig. 4-9 Leave as much of the original metal on the car as possible. The more you have left, the easier the repair will be.

have when you're done is a gaping hole surrounded by structurally sound metal, you've made the repair job a lot bigger than it had to be.

If the hole you made is too large, you won't have much of a guide to determine the shape of the metal piece you have to make. The result is that you'll wind up spending as much if not more time as the guys in Detroit do to recreate the original shape of the car.

REMOVING THE RUST

Even though you've grinded down the paint and are looking at bare metal, don't be fooled into thinking that all the rust has gone. You've only gotten rid of the rust you can see. The metal may look shiny and squeaky clean, but it's really rusting away in front of your eyes—you just can't see it.

At the risk of sounding like a TV ad for deodorant—way down deep in the metal there's still a problem, and you won't be able to solve it with the grinder. Rust is the result of a chemical reaction between the steel and the air. To be more scientific, the iron bonds with the oxygen to form ferric oxide—an $80 word for rust. The most common ways to reverse this reaction involve heat, chemistry, or both.

If you heat the metal, you'll force the oxygen out of the iron and stop the rusting process dead in its tracks. With enough heat, you can actually reverse the process and convert the rust back into iron. This might sound terrific, but there are two problems with it. Heating the metal to the point where the oxygen will be driven out involves temperatures that will damage the integrity of the steel and probably cause the metal to warp. Getting the metal hot enough to convert the rust to iron is called *smelting*. If you try to do it on your car, the metal will run like water. Unless you're planning some serious modifications to the shape and appearance of your car, this procedure is one you should avoid. At least get a bit more experience first.

A much easier way to solve the problem is a gift from the wonderful world of chemistry. You can release the oxygen trapped in the metal by starting a *redox* (reduction-oxidation) reaction. This mouthful of science is accomplished by washing the metal down with a mild acid. Several manufacturers make products for this purpose, and there's not much of a difference among them. You can use one of them to do the job. If you can't find any, check out your local camera store to see if they have any of the "stop" solutions used to process black-and-white film. Stop solutions are weak concentrations of acetic acid with a serious enough pH to do the job. You can also use muriatic acid; this stuff is sold in hardware stores and is used to clean brick and stone.

None of these acids is strong enough to turn your fingers to jelly, but that doesn't mean you shouldn't treat them with respect. Wear rubber gloves when you use any acid, and be sure to keep a supply of plain water around. If you splash some of this stuff in your eye, it's going to be really painful, and the best thing to do immediately is to wash your eye thoroughly with water. We all know that one of the cardinal rules of life is:

> **DON'T RUB IT IN**

That applies to your eyes as well as everything else. Read and pay attention to the instructions that come with the acid. It's a safe assumption that the manufacturer knows more than you do.

After you've washed down the metal with acid to remove the oxygen trapped in the surface, wash it again with plain water to get rid of the acid. You can't go any further until you have clean, neutralized metal in front of you. Once you've dried the metal thoroughly, you're ready to deal with the repair.

CHOOSING METAL FOR THE REPAIR

One of the main reasons for using metal to restore the surface is the strength of the material. Because a wide range of metal gauges is available, you have to decide what thickness of metal you'll use as a replacement. There are pluses and minuses here as well. You have to weigh the strength of the metal against the ease of working with it. Thick metal makes a repair that will probably outlast the rest of the car, but unless you're into heavy equipment, working with it is going to involve a lot of brain damage. A thin metal is a breeze to use, but it would be nice to have your work last long enough for you to show off to your friends and family. Somewhere between these two extremes is the right material.

The best guide is the gauge of the car's original metal. When you get right down to it, the best raw material for making the patch is a piece of metal from a similar car. You can probably find something in a junk yard. Your local parts store might also sell pieces of 20-gauge metal.

The metal you should use depends on your skill in metal working and the tools you have available. You're the only one who can make this decision.

The only absolute prohibition is that you must use the same type of metal that's on the car. There's a real temptation to use aluminum because it's strong, light, easy to work in heavy gauges. But using aluminum is a real no-no because the two metals will corrode each other wherever they're in contact. Any moisture that gets caught between them will act as an electrolyte, causing a chemical reaction similar to the way a battery works. Because the only places the two metals are in contact is where they're held together, you can imagine the consequences.

Before you can add new metal to the car, you first have to know exactly what metal to add. You can't simply cut out a piece of sheet metal and secure it to the car. Before you even touch the replacement metal, you have to know three things in this order:

1. How big a piece you'll need.
2. How the piece has to be shaped.
3. How it's going to be attached.

I suppose you could eyeball the damage, get a rough idea of how much metal you have to add, secure it to the car, and then trim it down after it's attached—but you'd just be making a lot of extra work for yourself. The right way—and the easier way—is to make a template for the replacement metal.

Cardboard is a good choice for making a template. You want it to be thick enough to hold a shape but thin enough to easily cut with a pair of scissors. Shirt cardboard, the kind you get from the laundry, is a good choice.

Make a rough approximation of the size you'll need and cut out a slightly larger piece of cardboard. Don't worry about matching the exact size because you'll trim it down as soon as you finish fitting it to the car. Place the cardboard

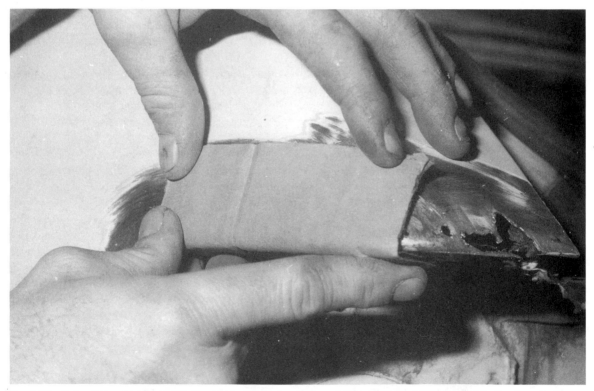

Fig. 4-10   Cut a piece of cardboard to the approximate size of the patch you have to make and fit it to the damaged area. Add a half inch or so of extra cardboard all around the repair.

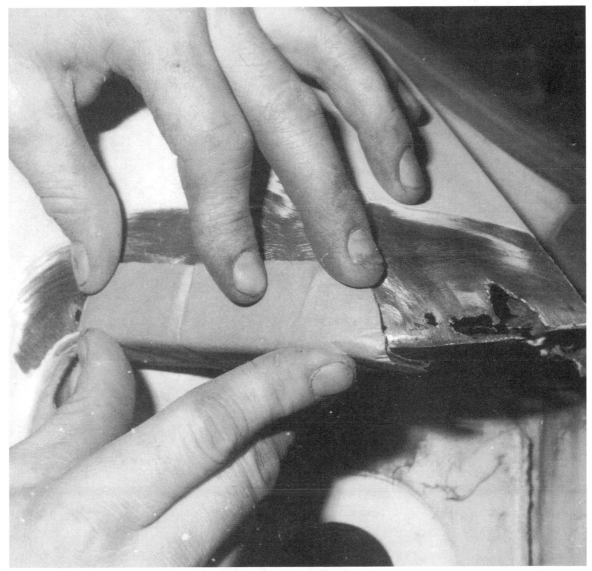

Fig. 4-11   Trim the cardboard one side at a time, making sure that all the edges and corners remain aligned with the car.

over the damaged area of the car and use a pen to mark the final size. You have to add an inch or so of cardboard around the periphery of the damage to provide room to attach the replacement metal to the car.

If the damage is located in an area that contains edges, fold the cardboard over the edge and leave at least half an inch of extra material after the fold. This is where you'll be attaching the new metal to the original metal remaining on the car.

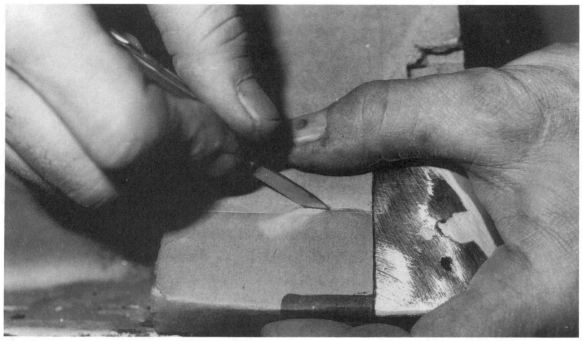

Fig. 4-12   You can mark the cardboard with a pencil and then cut it with a pair of scissors, or use a small knife to remove the excess cardboard while still holding it on the car.

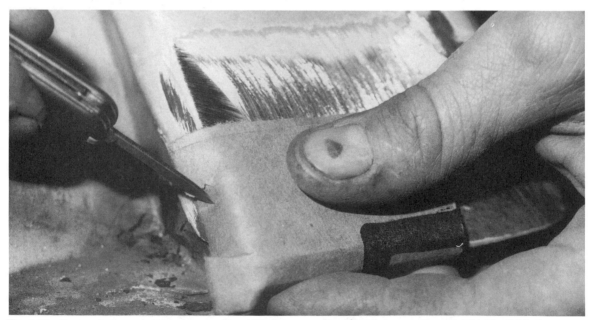

Fig. 4-13   Be sure to leave enough extra cardboard to give yourself sufficient room on the patch to attach it to the car.

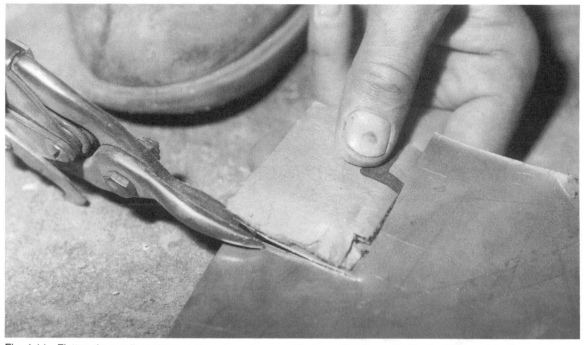

Fig. 4-14   Flatten the cardboard template and use it as a guide for cutting the metal blank to be used for the patch.

Fig. 4-15   Mark the locations of the edges on the metal and make the bends by using a hammer to bend the metal.

Fig. 4-16   Trim the metal to the size you marked with the template. Some bends are easier to make before the metal is cut to size.

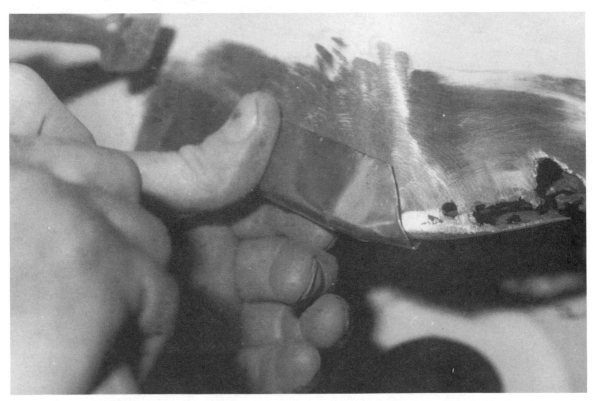

Fig. 4-17   Any final adjustments to the shape of the patch have to be made while holding the metal on the car.

After you make the cardboard template, flatten it out and trace its outline on the sheet metal you've gotten for the repair. If the replacement metal has any sharp bends in it, mark their locations on the metal when you finish tracing the outline so you'll know where to bend the metal.

Cut out the metal patch with a pair of shears or a small saw, and be careful to follow the outline. It's a bit of work to cut the metal, and you don't want to have to do it over again because you made a mistake cutting it out.

Position the flat piece of replacement metal over the damaged area on the car and, holding it securely in place, bend over all the folds you've marked. Don't try to get perfectly sharp edges on the bends; it's impossible to do that by hand. When you have a good idea of how the metal is going to fit on the car, you can take it off and use a hammer to bang the edges and corners into sharp folds.

You can make right-angle bends and sharp corners by putting the new metal on a piece of heavier metal and using it as a die. Hammer the sharp corners into the metal, stopping frequently to check the fit by putting the metal patch back on the car. Don't do too much shaping of the metal without checking. Metal bends pretty quickly, and it's a lot easier to bang the bend sharper than it is to flatten it out. And it's a big mistake to assume that you're aiming for a right-angle bend. Most of the bends you'll need will be anything but right angles.

UNDERCOATING

Once you have an acceptable fit and are ready to put the new metal on the car, you might want to think about coating the bare metal that's going to be trapped under the patch. Even though you'll be covering the repair with Bondo, primer, and so on, some spots will remain completely uncovered. If you're covering a hole in the car, you should also think about the original metal surrounding the damaged area. You've ground away the rust and rot, but the metal left around the damage has probably been thinned by the rust, too.

Several products are designed to prevent metal from rusting. If you don't have any of them around, you can use primer because it adheres well to bare metal. While it's true that some of the other products do a better job, remember that the metal is going to be sealed behind several layers of Bondo, primer, putty, and paint. If you do this repair properly, once you cover the repair, the metal will never see the light of day. This is the time to protect it.

If you're covering a hole, you also have the chance to get a look behind the metal and make sure it's protected as well. Because the back of the metal is probably covered with something—undercoating, dirt, factory prime, etc.—you can't expect to cover it with a quick coat of primer. If the hole is large enough for you to get back there and clean it off, you can use any available product as a protective coating. If you can't reach inside the hole, there are several oil-based products you can use. These will soak through whatever loose debris is covering the back of the metal and give it at least some measure of protection.

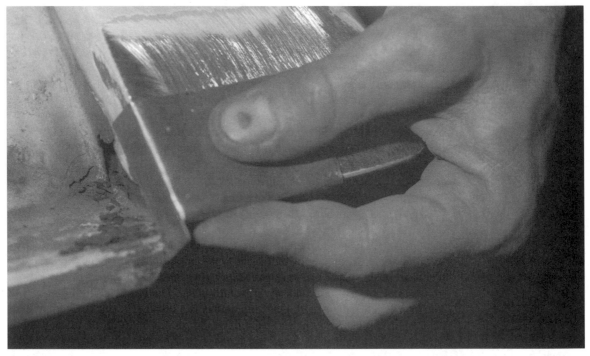

Fig. 4-18   Extra metal at the corners of the patch should be bent over rather than removed because they can only make the patch stronger.

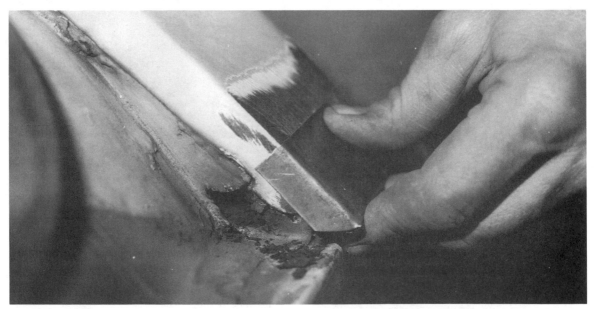

Fig. 4-19   The completed patch should fit snugly all around the damage with enough extra metal to attach it to the car.

POP RIVETING

The hardest part of fitting the new metal to the body is putting in the first pop rivet. Put the metal patch on the car and carefully get it into position. If you have a sharp corner or bend in the patch, use that as the starting point to line up the patch. You can adjust the rest of the fit later.

Once you're sure of the fit, you'll find it easier to drill the holes in the patch before you attach it to the car. Lay the metal on a piece of wood, and make the holes for the pop rivets. You might want to use a few pieces of masking tape to help hold it there. Drill a hole through the patch and the body of the car, making sure the patch doesn't move out of position while you drill the hole. You need to apply a lot of pressure on the drill in order to go through the metal. Consequently, the drill bits have a nasty habit of snapping when you least expect it. It's a good idea to make a short bit, as explained in chapter 3 and reserve it for use in drilling pop-rivet holes.

The first rivets you put in should be in the four corners of the patch because they will keep the metal from moving as you put in the rest of the rivets. After you secure the patch with the first pop rivet, remove the tape you put on to hold the metal in position, and check the alignment of the metal patch before you add the rest of the pop rivets. You can probably move the patch slightly as long as

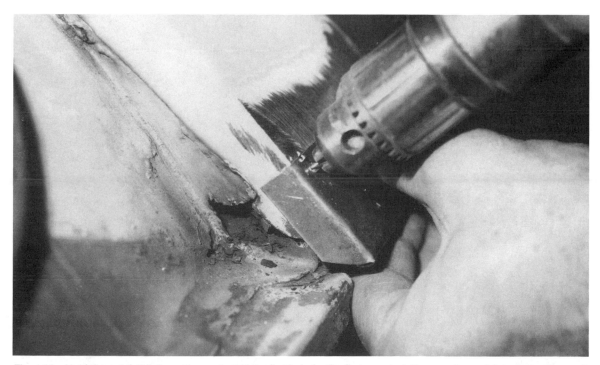

Fig. 4-20 Hold the patch tightly on the car to drill the first hole for the first pop rivet. If you make a mistake here, the patch won't fit properly on the car.

Fig. 4-21   Putting in the first pop rivet will hold the patch securely in position for the rest of the pop rivets.

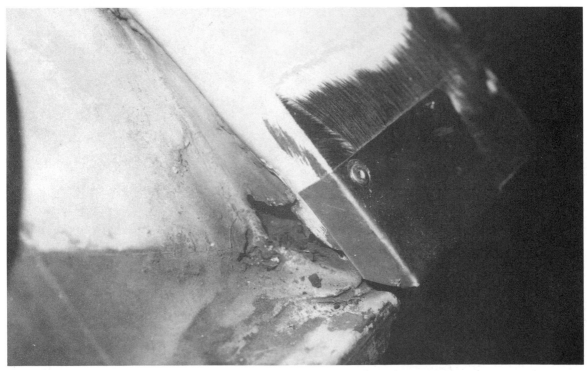

Fig. 4-22   Once the first pop rivet is done, you can see how the patch will fit on the car.

it's only being held on with one rivet, but the more rivets you add, the less you'll be able to shift its position. After all, the reason you're riveting it in position is so it can't move at all.

The number of rivets you should use to secure the patch to the car depends on several things—how large a patch you're making, how many bends it has, and so on. The rivets should be put on wherever the new metal overlaps the original metal. The larger the patch, the further apart you can put the rivets, but you should place them at least every inch or so. Work your way around the periphery of the patch, and keep putting in rivets until you get back to the starting point.

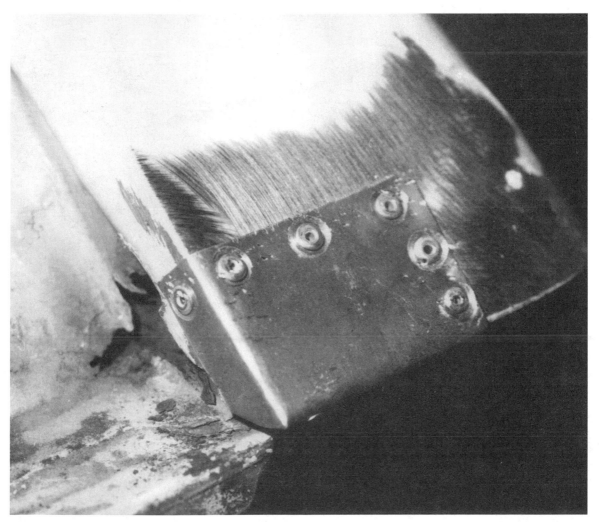

Fig. 4-23   The number of rivets you should use depends on the size of the patch. Since we're not welding the metal, use enough rivets to guarantee that the patch won't lift off the car.

When you have this sort of work done in a body shop, the rivets are put in much further apart because their only purpose is to hold the patch in place so it can be welded to the car body afterwards. A welded repair is a lot stronger than one that's done only with rivets, but welding isn't something you can learn from a book. The only way to get good with a welding torch is to put in the time welding. In addition, the metal you're using on the car can only be worked with the kind of heat generated by a welding torch—the propane torches you buy in a hardware store are good for a lot of jobs, but they don't produce the temperatures you need to work even the thinner steel now being used on most new

Fig. 4-24   Make sure to put rivets on all sides of the patch so the corners of the metal will fit snugly against the car body.

cars. If you want to have the patch welded to the car and you've never done any welding before, take the car to a body shop and have someone do it for you. It will cost a couple of bucks to have done, but it's going to be a lot less than the price of the welding outfit you would have to buy to do it yourself. And you won't be running the risk of ruining the repair you worked so hard to do.

Now that you have secured the new metal to the body, you have to prepare the surface for finishing. The first thing to do is to make sure there's room for the Bondo. Examine the repair and mark any part of it that's higher than the original surface. Use a hammer to bang down the patch and leave enough of a

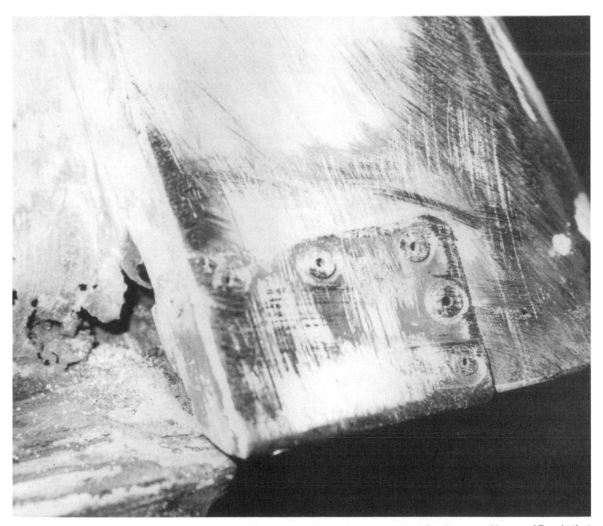

Fig. 4-25   The tops of the rivets have to be below the surface of the metal to leave room for the several layers of Bondo that follow. This can be done by a combination of banging and grinding.

depression to hold the Bondo you're going to add. You'll probably find that you have to do a lot of hammering on the edges, corners, and ends because those areas will have overlapping metal. Make sure the rivets are also below the level of the surrounding surface.

It's impossible to judge height and depth correctly by eye. The surface has several different pieces of metal on it, so it's easy for the eye to be fooled. The only way to be sure of the depth is to feel it with the palm of your hand and check the contour with a straightedge, just as described in chapter 2.

USING FIBERGLASS-REINFORCED BONDO

Once you have riveted the metal patch to the car body and you've hammered it below the line of the original metal, you can think of the rest of the job as repairing a simple dent. The only difference is that you should use fiberglass-reinforced Bondo—the super Bondo we talked about earlier—instead of the stuff used on the dent as described in the last chapter.

Super Bondo is stronger, has more body, and is also waterproof. This last quality is important because you don't want water to seep below the finished surface and get caught between the original metal and the patch. If that happens, it's only going to be a matter of time before cracks start appearing, rust starts again, and all the Bondo begins lifting off the repair.

The fiberglass-reinforced Bondo is more expensive than the regular variety, but the difference in price is far outweighed by the advantages it gives you, especially when you're repairing damage caused by rust and rot. Super Bondo comes in the same two-part form as regular Bondo and is mixed, applied, and worked in the same way with the same tools.

If the holes caused by the rust or rot are fairly small, you can use the super Bondo to fill them without first making a metal patch to cover the holes. The fiberglass-reinforced Bondo isn't as strong as metal, but it's significantly stronger than the regular Bondo we used on the dent as described in chapter 3.

You're the only one who can judge whether you have to add metal to the car, but if the original metal still has a good deal of strength to it, a super Bondo only repair is perfectly adequate. Regardless of the integrity of the remaining metal, however, there are a few cases in which metal should still be used. You'll have to add some metal to the car if there are holes in the car body that extend around corners and edges, or if there's metal missing that's needed as support for trim, lights, and so on. It might not be necessary to cover the entire area with new metal because there are several products on the market designed to deal with exactly this problem.

You can buy flexible metal edging and prefabricated metal corners in most auto-body supply stores. Of course these will still have to be riveted or welded to the body, but that's still less work than having to make the metal yourself. If you've ever done any work with plaster or wallboard, you might be familiar with similar products used to create hard corners on walls. They're nailed to the corner studs in much the same way that the body-repair edging gets riveted to the body. Besides giving the corner a lot of strength, it provides a clean edge when you're applying the Bondo.

When you're using super Bondo alone to fill in a hole, make sure you don't end up with most of the material inside the hole or beneath the surface of the car. This is a waste of Bondo and time because you'll just have to mix more material and do the job over again.

It's not difficult to cover a hole with fiberglass-reinforced Bondo as I mentioned earlier, it has a lot more body than the standard Bondo. You can't avoid having some of the material fall under the surface, but the fiberglass filaments in the Bondo will make it tend to hold a flat shape, even when it's still soft.

When you start putting the material on the surface, don't begin by laying the soft Bondo over the hole. Put a bunch of material on the applicator and lay it on some of the solid metal surrounding the hole you want to cover. Without using a lot of pressure, smear the Bondo over the hole, making sure there's more than enough Bondo available to cover the hole. Even though this stuff has a good deal of body to it, you have to put it on thicker than the standard Bondo when you're using it to cover a hole.

Fig. 4-26   Fiberglass-reinforced Bondo can't be applied neatly. Work it into the holes with a putty knife and worry about the excess when it hardens.

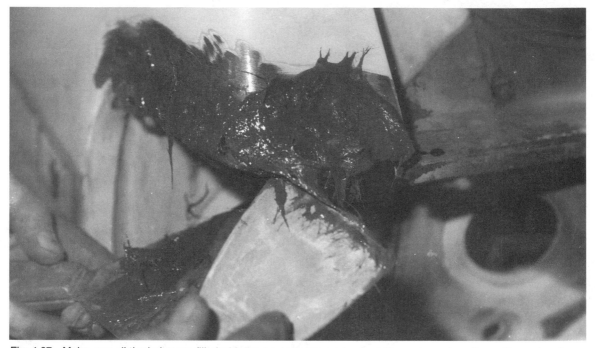

Fig. 4-27 Make sure all the holes are filled with the super Bondo and extend the coverage over the entire work area.

When you apply the Bondo to the surface, spread it around with minimal hand pressure against the surface. Remember that the more pressure you use, the thinner the coat is going to be, and you need a fairly thick coat to cover the hole. Cover all of the work area, just as you did in repairing the dent discussed in chapter 3, and give the Bondo a few minutes to harden.

Once the Bondo has hardened enough to be worked with the cheese grater, you can follow the same procedures outlined in chapter 3 to finish it off. When you've finished sanding the super Bondo and are ready to put on the second coat, use regular Bondo instead of the fiberglass-reinforced material. Although the fiberglass material is stronger than the regular Bondo, the fine hairs of the fiberglass will tend to stick up and make it just about impossible to get a surface smooth enough for the primer and paint. You might not be able to see the fiberglass hairs while the surface is still rough, but they will become painfully obvious when you paint and polish later.

One good reason for only using the fiberglass-reinforced Bondo when you absolutely have to is that fiberglass can be very nasty stuff. If you get any of the fibers under your skin, they're going to be really painful, and it's murder to remove them. Because the individual fibers are very thin, they're difficult to see and even more difficult to grab with a pair of tweezers. You won't know the meaning of the word ''annoying'' until you spend an hour trying to remove something from under your skin that you can feel but can't see.

Fig. 4-28   The fiberglass strands in the super Bondo give the material its strength but also cause the surface to be very uneven and unsuitable for painting.

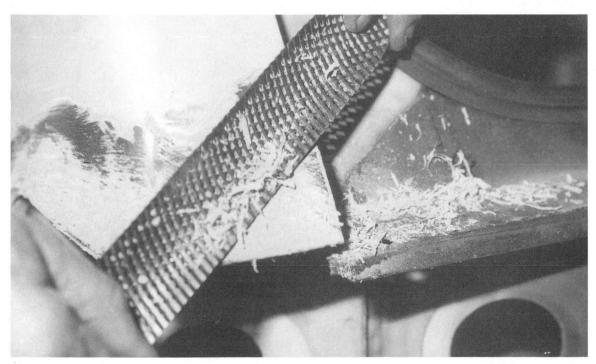

Fig. 4-29   Cut the Bondo with a cheese grater, just as you did in the last chapter.

Fig. 4-30   When you finish with the cheese grater, the material will be rougher than the surface left by the regular Bondo at that same stage of repair.

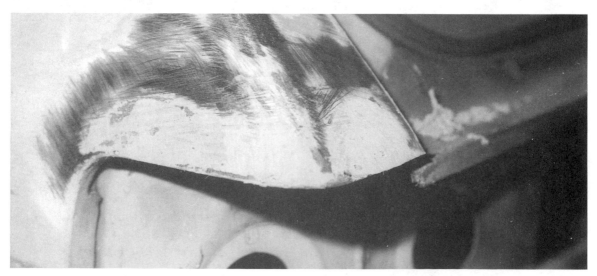

Fig. 4-31   The sanded finish on the super Bondo will be smoother, but the fine hairs of fiberglass will show through paint. Use a coat of regular Bondo to cover the sanded surface of the super Bondo.

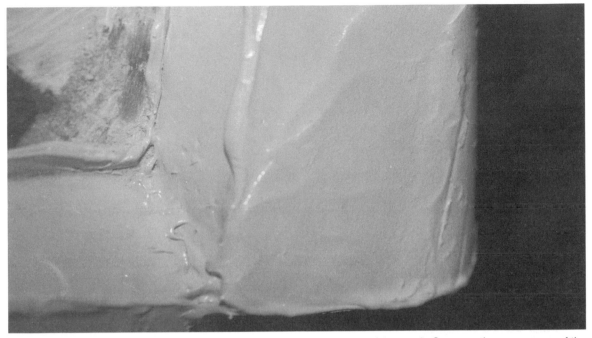

Fig. 4-32   A coat of regular Bondo will form a good foundation for the rest of the repair. Compare the appearance of the regular Bondo in the photograph to the appearance of the super Bondo shown in Figure 4-30.

FINISHING THE REPAIR

All the steps you need to do from here on to prepare the surface for painting are exactly the same ones we went through in repairing the dent. You have to do the same kind of sanding and priming with exactly the same materials. The work is no different just because you're repairing damage due to rust or rot.

The steps involved in any kind of body repair—no matter what the damage—are always the same. Different jobs may start out further up or down the ladder, but the idea behind the work never changes. You go from working directly with the metal and making major changes in its shape or content to adding progressively finer layers of material to make the surface match the contour and finish of the original. As always, the first thing you have to do is examine the damage to get a reasonable idea of the amount of work in front of you.

The more experience you get in doing body work, the more accurately you'll be able to judge the amount of work needed for a repair. One of the reasons this is so important is that some repairs aren't worth the time it's going to take to do them. I'm not talking about whether or not to junk the car; I'm referring to the fact that some surfaces might be so damaged that they should really be replaced instead of being repaired. Twisted metal can only be straightened so much without a serious weakening of the metal, and a severely rotted area might not even have enough metal left to patch.

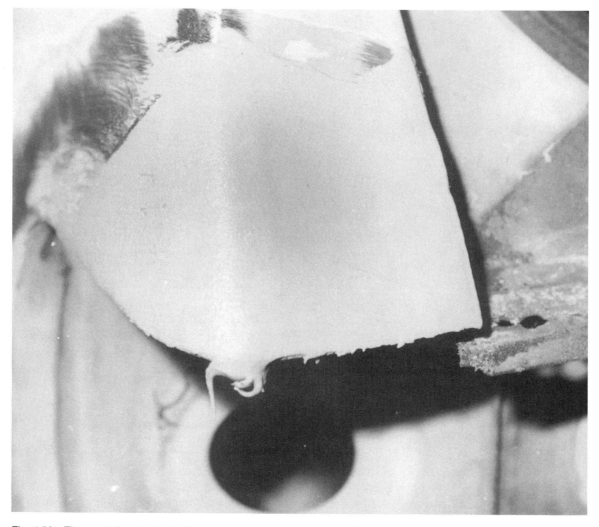

Fig. 4-33 The second coat of plain Bondo has to completely cover the fiberglass-reinforced Bondo.

Whether to repair or replace is always a hard call to make because there are usually a lot of variables involved. If you're dealing with a car that's either classic or old, it might be almost impossible to get replacement parts. If that's the case, you'll just have to work with what you have, no matter how bad the damage happens to be. The same argument holds if the replacement parts are expensive and you're working on a limited budget or—as sometimes happens— no budget at all. Finally, some repairs are just impossible to do yourself. For example, if the frame of the car is twisted or damaged, it's going to take a lot more than a hammer to straighten it.

Fig. 4-34 After cutting the Bondo with the cheese grater, sand it with progressively finer paper as described in Chapter 3.

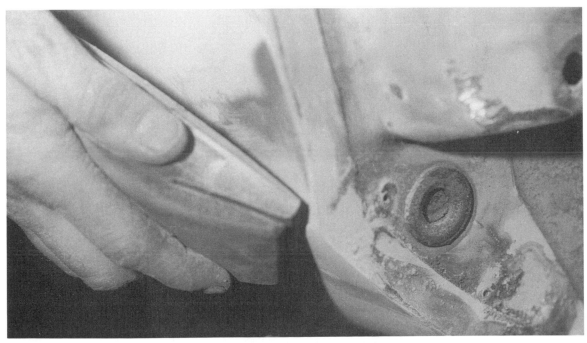

Fig. 4-35 Use a sanding block to reproduce the original contour of the metal.

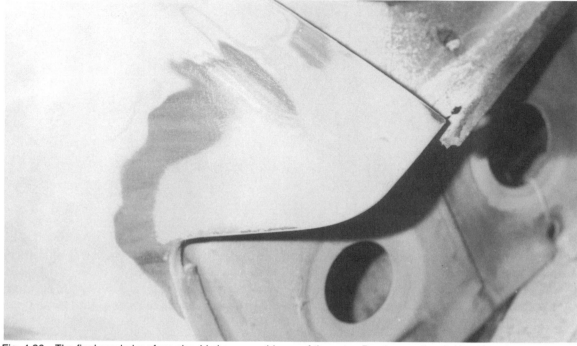

Fig. 4-36   The final sanded surface should show no evidence of the super Bondo covering the metal on the car.

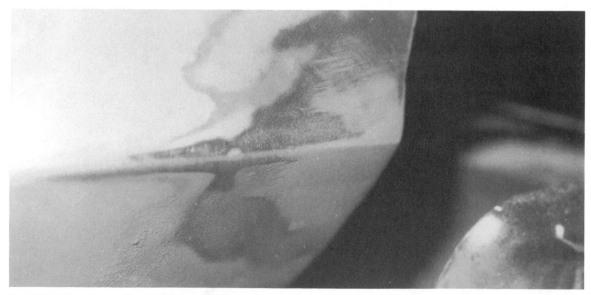

Fig. 4-37   The edges and curves of the original car body should be matched by sanding with the Bondo. The scratches left from the fine paper will be covered by the glazing putty.

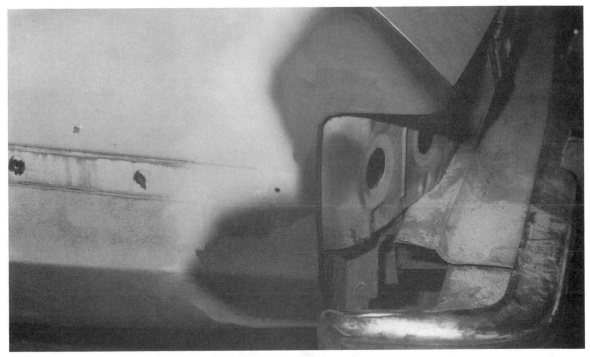

Fig. 4-38   Prime the work area to prepare it for the glazing putty.

The bottom line is that you have to be realistic when you find yourself facing a repair. Underestimating the damage can be just as big a mistake as overestimating your ability. No one believes in the power of positive thinking more than I do, but it's unfortunately true that you need a lot more than good vibes and high-grade karma when you decide to transform a car from an eyesore to an eyefull.

The real key to successful body work is experience. The more you do the more you'll be able to do. Nobody wants to spend hours and hours working on a repair and have the result look both awful and evident. As you get a handle on the skills needed to repair the car, you'll be able to successfully deal with heavier and more severe damage.

So be realistic when you first consider doing the entire repair by yourself. Weigh the degree of damage against the level of your ability, and have a body shop do the things you can't do. When you finally roll the finished product out of the garage and people come from far and wide to admire it, nobody's going to point out the parts you had done and the parts you did yourself. It's going to look terrific, and that's all anyone's going to remember. Trying to do more than you can will only result in a bad repair if you're lucky, and a bad injury if you're not.

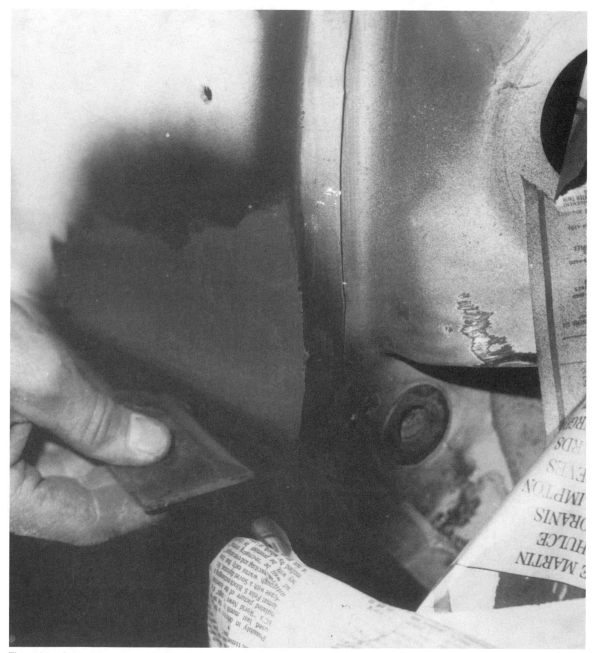

Fig. 4-39   Apply the glazing putty following the same procedure used in the last chapter.

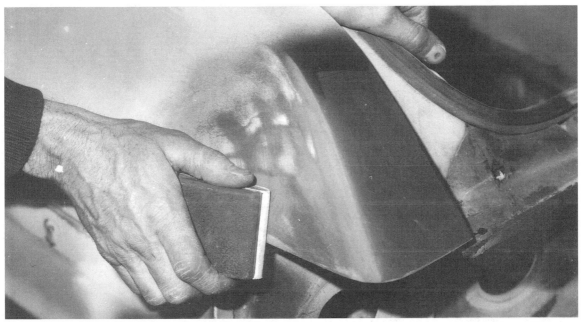

Fig. 4-40   Sand the putty with a sanding block and fine paper.

Fig. 4-41   It's easy to oversand edges, so pay particular attention to them and be careful when you're working on them.

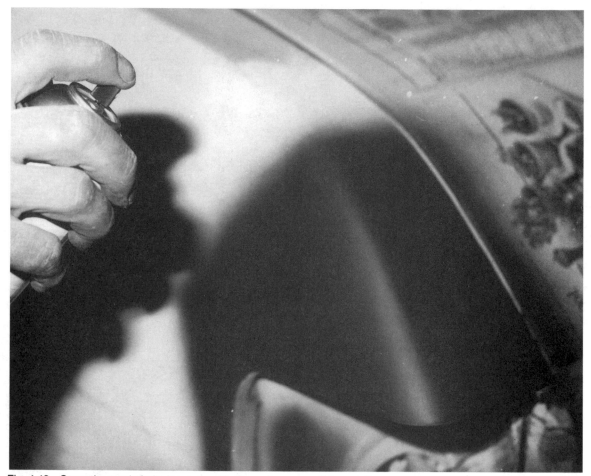

Fig. 4-42   Cover the sanded glazing putty with primer to prepare it for painting.

5
CHAPTER

Painting the Surface

FINALLY PAINTING THE CAR—THIS IS IT. AFTER LOTS OF WORK AND BRAIN DAM-age—to say nothing about cuts and bruises—you've reached the point in the repair where it all comes together. The hours you've spent banging, pulling, and sanding—every single one of them—have been aimed at getting to this point. But don't think you can relax. The feeling of accomplishment that comes from watching the paint cover your repair is really terrific, but there's no such thing as a free lunch. Remember, the more you want to gain, the more you have to risk.

You would think that covering the repair with paint would be a nice, simple operation, and—if you still believe in the tooth fairy—you can go on believing that. I hate to be the one to shatter your illusions, but unfortunately, painting the car is at least as complex a procedure as anything you've done so far—and the consequences of making a mistake are a lot more serious.

The word ''serious'' means different things to different people. Nothing you do to the surface of your car is going to end the world as we know it, so you don't have to worry about that. On the other hand, a simple slip of the wrist can put you back at the putty and sanding stage, and that would force you to do a lot of work over again and probably generate a lot of anger and frustration. Conse-quently, you'd be shaping the repair with less than a cool head and a pure heart, and you'd more than likely get a bit careless and take off some essential skin along with the nonessential putty. Putty or primer would get into the injury and cause an infection, and you'd spend two weeks with your hands wrapped in ban-dages. I'd call that pretty serious.

Everything you've done so far has been designed to be hidden under a final coat of paint. If you mess up with the Bondo or get some runs with the primer, the worst that can happen is that you'll have to do a bit of sanding to smooth off the surface. Even though that's always a somewhat tedious job, the most it can cost you is a few hours or so of work because all the materials dry or harden quickly. Now that you're dealing with paint, however, things are very different.

Paint takes time to dry; the exact amount of time depends on the kind of paint, the temperature of the air, how it's applied, and so on. When you make a mistake at this stage of the game, the best that can happen is that you'll lose some time—much more time than would be caused by a mistake earlier in the repair. The worst that can happen is pretty severe. Overspraying can mean a lot of rubbing and the possibility of ruining the paint in the undamaged areas of the car. Paint changes color as it dries, and if you're not careful about matching the color, you might wind up painting the car over and over again.

But let's not get into painting with a negative attitude. We've managed to get this far and—hey, you only live once or twice, so let's do it.

PREPARING THE CAR

Before you even think about painting the repair, the work area has to be masked off. This is the same sort of paper-and-tape covering you did when you sprayed the car with primer. But, because this is paint, not primer, you have to look at the job differently. When you sprayed primer on the car, all you had to cover was the work area because the purpose of the primer is to put a seal over the Bondo and putty. Primer is similar to paint in application, but the reason for applying it is obviously very different.

No matter how careful you are about matching the color, you can't avoid having differences between old and new paint. Even if the color is an exact match, the old paint has been exposed to the ravages of industrial America for much longer; the sun has changed its color; atmospheric pollutants have played havoc with the pigment and surface. Even repeated washing or waxing has had an effect on the appearance of the car.

When I bought my car in 1968, I was given a can of touch-up paint that came from the same batch used to paint the car. Three years or so later, I opened it up for the first time to cover a few nicks, and there was an obvious difference in color. The moral is that you can only be guaranteed of a perfect color match when the paint is still fresh. Aging is cruel.

Your chances of perfectly matching the color and texture are really non-existent so you have to apply the new paint in a way that makes the difference between it and the original invisible to the eye. The only way to do this is to avoid creating places where there will be a hard line between the new and old paint. When you apply the new paint to the car, you have to blend it into the old paint. The differences will still be there, but because they're spread out over a wider area, you won't be able to see them. While this technique works really well for hiding the color difference, the difference in texture and finish will have to be handled by the methods you use to polish the new paint.

Blending the two paints means putting thinner and thinner layers of new paint on the car in widening circles around the repair. It also means that you'll

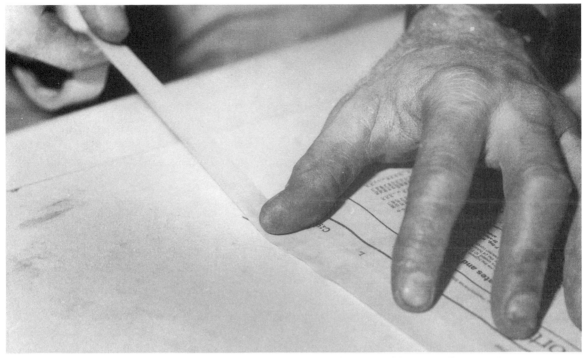

Fig. 5-1   Apply the tape to the edge of the paper used to mask the car leaving half the width of the tape free to stick to the car.

Fig. 5-2   Always put the paper on panel ends or definite contour lines on the car. This will help minimize slight differences in paint color.

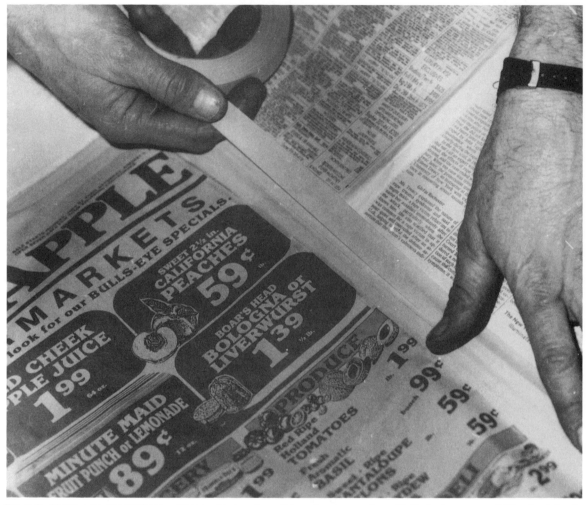

Fig. 5-3 Using a double thickness of tape wherever two pieces of paper overlap will eliminate any possibility of paint getting in through the seams.

be working on a larger area than you had been during all the steps leading up to the painting. When you mark out the area to be masked off, put the tape at least a foot or so beyond the edges of the repair. You can go further if you want, or if the particular geometry of your car requires it. There's no maximum limit to the area you can paint but, as you can see, there is a minimum.

The best way to minimize the difference between old and new paint is to put the tape on the car in such a way that you'll be working on complete body panel or, second best, along a line in the contour of the car body—anywhere there is a sculpted rim, lip, piece of trim, or anything that runs the length of the damaged panel. If the tape runs along a body line or on the edge of the adjoining body panel, the minimum amount of new paint will follow the contour of the car body and help make the difference between the old and new paint as invisible as possible.

Blending new paint onto old paint is called "drifting the paint," and it is essentially an exercise in creating an optical illusion. The work area has the full intensity of the new paint—it's the only paint that's on the surface. As you move out to the surrounding areas, you're putting on progressively thinner layers of new paint. Two inches or so from the edge of the repair, you might have equal amounts of new and old paint. Four inches from the edge, the proportion might change to 20% new paint and 80% old paint. This thinning should continue until there's no new paint at all on the surface.

If you do it correctly, drifting the new paint into the old can make the difference between the two paint colors completely invisible. It's not difficult to thin the new paint at the edges, but the degree to which the final edge is invisible depends, to a large extent, on where the final edge is located. Again, the best place to end the final layer of new paint is, at a definite line on the car body. Trying to make the final drift point in the middle of a plain surface is much harder to do successfully.

Mask off the area to be painted just as you did when you were preparing to spray on the primer. Outline the area with masking tape and put on the taped

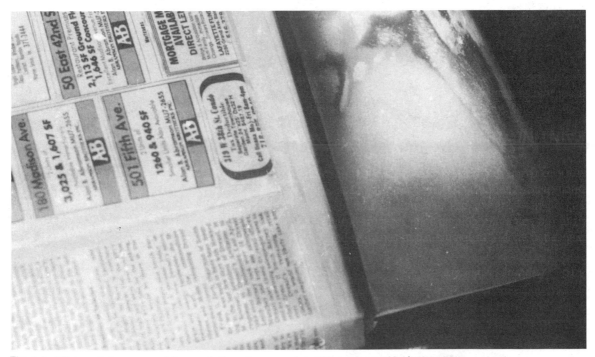

Fig. 5-4 When painting a complete panel, the extra space for drifting the panel isn't necessary.

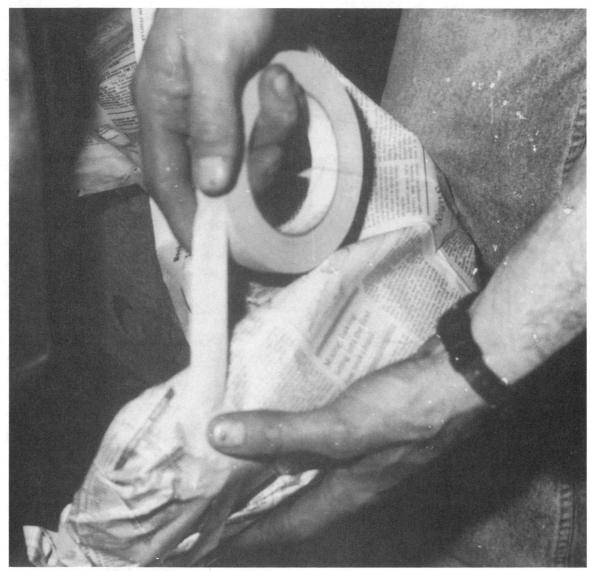

Fig. 5-5   Wrap the bumpers in paper and run tape around them to hold the paper securely.

paper. Be particularly careful with any hard edges you want to keep such as the edges around windows, trim, lights, door locks, handles, and so on. Use at least a double thickness of tape on these so you can be as sure as possible that paint won't get on them.

When you mask off small areas, such as chrome keyholes, put the edge of the tape at the point where the chrome meets the body of the car but leave a 1/16 inch or so of chrome showing. The idea is to wind up with a thin line of paint on the chrome so you don't damage the edge of the paint when you remove the tape. Lifting tape off wet paint can cause the paint to pull off the car body. However, if you wait until the paint is thoroughly dry and then peel the tape off, there's a good chance it will pull chips off the body.

Because you can easily damage the paint when you remove the tape, you want to keep the tape edge away from the area you're painting. This is why you have to be very careful where you put it on and how you take it off. Once you go through the paint job, we'll talk about the best ways to get the tape off the car. For the moment, however, let's concentrate on putting it on correctly.

As you wrap the tape around the chrome, keep your eye only on the edge of the chrome. The more care you take here, the less work you'll have to do later, when you've finished painting the car. When the tape is completely wrapped around the chrome, press it against the center of the keyhole and add a few layers on top of that to be sure.

Don't forget to cover the tires. These are a real pain in the neck to cover with paper but there is an alternative. Most hardware stores sell large plastic dropcloths that do the job perfect. As a matter of fact, it's a good idea to get a bunch of these because you can use them to mask off the floor and walls while you're working on the car. If you want to keep the floor free from paint spattering, move the car out of the way, lay one or more of these cloths on the ground, and drive the car on top of it.

Fig. 5-6   Let the paper drape over the tires and cover them. If you're painting right to the edges of the metal panel surrounding the tires, use a separate plastic dropcloth to cover them.

Fig. 5-7   To keep unwanted paint droplets off the masked areas of the car, let the paper go at least two feet into the protected areas.

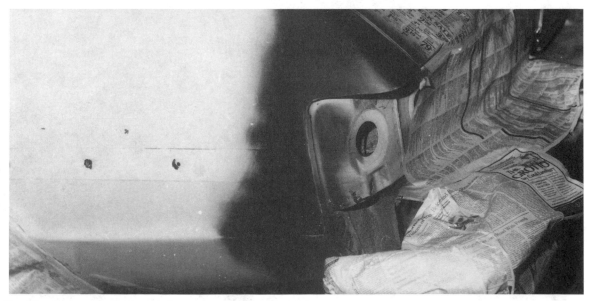

Fig. 5-8   Areas under lights and trim can be painted since they'll be covered when the lights and trim are put back on the car.

It takes a bit of practice to control the area the paint is going to cover when you put it on the car, and even a lot of experience is no guarantee that paint droplets aren't going to show up on the car a considerable distance from the work area. Once you move the car, you should consider covering the rest of the car with plastic sheets. The sheets only cost a few bucks and can be reused—and anything that makes your life easier is a good thing.

Don't be in a rush to mask off the car. While everyone knows that the quality of a repair is judged by the final appearance of the paint you put on the car, that judgment is also tempered by the paint you managed to keep off the car. Neatness counts.

CHOOSING THE PAINT

By the time you reach a certain age, you learn that there are no real guarantees in life. Even the absolutely unconditional, written-in-stone, no-questions-asked guarantees that you find here and there are loaded with so many disclaimers, written in such legalese, or printed in such flea type that you just know the manufacturer's going to have some way to squirm out of them.

Remember this: There's no way you're going to be able to buy paint that exactly matches the color of your car—Guaranteed. The hook here is that you can probably get paint that's close. The starting point for matching paint is the manufacturer's paint number. Each color that comes out of the factory is a precise mix of pigments according to a strictly defined formula. If you take a trip to your local paint shop and give them the make, model, year, and color of your car, you stand a good chance of getting a can of paint that's an acceptable match. Paint manufacturers go to considerable lengths to use similar pigments and tight quality controls when they mix paint designed to be the same as those mixed by the car manufacturers.

But as we've already seen, paint starts to change color as soon as it's put on the car, so you know that getting the original color is going to result in a mismatch. There's no way to get around this short of painting the entire car, so your goal is to get paint that comes as close as possible to the original.

If you're afraid that the color of your car has changed a great deal since it first rolled off the assembly line, your best bet is to take a sample of the car's paint to the paint store. Hunt around your car to see if there's a small painted part of the body you can easily remove and bring with you. Fenders and hoods are obviously out of the question, but something like the flap over the gas tank is a good choice.

At the paint shop, you'll probably find chip charts of the available colors. It's a real temptation to use them as the way to pick the color you want; you might even be able to borrow them and bring them to the car. You can use these charts, but you should be aware that the colors shown on them might not be the same as the colors of the actual paint. Many chip charts are made with ink, not paint, so the color and texture on the chip chart is often nothing more than a close approximation of the paint color and finish. You can use them as a guide, but you could easily be fooling yourself if you think of them as the final word.

When you buy the paint, you have to give some thought to how much of it you want to buy. Obviously, the larger the repair, the more paint you'll need, but there's no way you'll be able to buy exactly enough paint to cover the repair. In the best of all possible worlds, you would pour the last bit of paint out of the can to cover the last bit of the repair. The real world, however, is quite different.

It would be a colossal mistake, even if it were possible, to buy only the exact quantity of paint you need. Not only are no two colors ever exactly the same, but the color will be slightly different every time it's mixed. The greater the number of different pigments in the color, the smaller the chance that the same proportions will be used every time the color is mixed. And don't think for a minute that slight changes in pigment won't really be visible. Everything depends on the color of the pigment you vary.

My car is British Racing Green—a combination of green, yellow, black, and white. Slight changes in the amount of black or white will affect the brightness of the color and differences in the amount of yellow or green will affect the color itself. Once I had a quart of paint mixed to do a repair and a bit too much yellow was used in the mix. The difference was so great, I couldn't use the paint. Drifting the paint will minimize a shift in color, but there are limits to what drifting can do.

If you get paint mixed for your car, make sure to get some extra paint (a quart is plenty). That's the only way you can be sure you'll have paint that's a perfect match for the paint you'll be using in the repair. You'll always have a use for the extra paint, too, because every repair requires touching up, patching, and even occasional respraying.

There's no hard-and-fast rule to tell you how much paint you're going to need. There are just too many variables—the size of the repair, the number of coats, the kind of paint, even the type of equipment you'll be using to put it on the car. If you have to make a guess, judge it against the estimate that a quart of paint is usually enough to cover a whole side on a medium-sized car. You can ask the people in the paint store to give you an idea of how much paint you'll need, but remember that they're more interested in selling paint than selling enough paint.

A few other things you'll have to buy are thinner, clear coat, and some (optional) paint additives. Because there are several types of paint—enamel, lacquer, acrylics, and so on—there are also different varieties of thinners. Thinners are definitely not all the same. Make sure you get the thinner that's recommended for the type of paint you'll be using. The amount of thinner you'll need for the paint will be mentioned on the paint-can label. All auto body paint has to be thinned before it is used. While there are occasionally reasons for not following the paint manufacturer's thinning recommendations, you've got to learn the rules before you start breaking them. The recommended thinning directions might not be absolutely ideal for the job you're doing, but they're a lot better than an uneducated guess.

In the last several years, clear coat has become a popular way to put a finish on a car. Once upon a time, the car got painted and, once it was dry, it was polished down to the desired degree of smoothness.

This has changed. Most modern paint jobs use the paint only as pigment. Its job is to color the car—nothing more. Once enough coats of paint have been put on to reach the desired color intensity, several layers of a clear coat—simply a colorless, transparent paint—are sprayed on to protect the paint and provide a surface for polishing. Painting like this means a bit more work, but there are some good reasons for doing it.

From the point of view of chemistry, separating the paint and the finish means manufacturers can optimize the designs of both the paint and the clear. Because only the clear coat is polished and exposed to the atmosphere, it can be chemically engineered to be as hard and inert as necessary. On the other hand, the only consideration that has to be given to the design of the paint is intensity, purity, and any other things that will make the color as fade-free and permanent as possible. Because these two considerations are often contradictory, splitting the paint process can give you the best of both worlds.

Just as there are recommendations for the thinner, there are recommendations for the type of clear coat to use with each type of paint. Follow the recommendations because while an improper mix might look terrific in the beginning, some severe problems can show up after time. Remember that the paint and the clear coat take a long time to dry completely, and they both change chemically throughout the drying process. Using the wrong clear coat can cause things like blistering, peeling, discoloring, etc., to appear over the long term. If you've gone through a lot of work to do a repair, it's a real bummer to watch it self-destruct a few months later.

Play it safe. Choosing, mixing, applying, and finishing the paint is the most complex part of a repair. The people who make the paint have gone through a lot of work to provide a range of chemicals designed to give satisfactory results—but only if you follow their recommendations. There are always tricks and special techniques that can be used to make things a bit easier, but—unless you know exactly what you're doing—you will probably wind up with a disaster if you try to use them. It's all your call, but keep in mind the undisputed fact that the consequences of breaking the rules are lopsided—you'll either make things a little bit better or a whole lot worse.

Before we leave the subject of choosing paint, be warned that on your first trip to the paint shop you will face a huge array of merchandise. You'll find lots of small containers labeled with "accelerator," "hardener," and so on. All this stuff is great for particular purposes but you're better off ignoring them until you get a better understanding of how the paint should be handled. Chemical additives that cause changes in the drying rate or the hardness of the finish are only good (or needed) if the intrinsic characteristics of the paint have to be changed, and there's just no way to tell that without being familiar with the paint in the first place. Try them out on your second or third repair, but not the first one you've ever done.

Just about the only additive you should think about buying is a paint adhesion promoter. This is a chemical that helps the paint stick to the surface. While you can sand the primer to provide a slightly rough surface for the new paint, you can't sand the areas where you're going to drift the new paint into the old paint. The adhesive will help the paint bond to the smooth surface you've left on the old paint. Just be sure you get the additive designed to work with the paint you're buying.

You should pick up some other supplies during your visit to the paint shop. Things like paper strainers and mixing sticks are often free of charge—or at least inexpensive—so you should stock up on them. They don't take up much room and, besides that, you'd be surprised how many of them you go through while you're painting, no matter how small the repair.

The bottom line for getting the paint and clear coat you need is to estimate the quantity, match the color to the car, and base the required amount of thinner and hardener by following the directions on the paint cans. And don't forget the free stuff.

PREPARING THE SURFACE FOR PAINT

The most careful paint job in the world will turn to total ruin if the surface wasn't properly prepared beforehand. Remember that the only way the paint can be expected to cover the car with color is if it can stick to the surface in the first place. Even though the chemistry of the paint is designed to adhere to just about anything—something you'll discover when you clean up—you have to help it a bit by getting the surface ready.

Before you even think about putting paint on the car, you have to clean the surface thoroughly. Every single bit of grease and dirt has to be removed from the work area. Dirt will show through the finish, and paint just won't stick to grease. Although you can buy special chemicals to clean the surface, any good wax remover will do the job. Just make sure that it doesn't contain oil or any other chemical that will leave a residue. The surface provided by primer is designed to hold paint, so anything sitting on top of it will cause problems.

If the old paint you plan to drift into the new paint is oxidized, clean it and rub it down with compound to get rid of all the dead paint. There's a considerable difference in color when paint oxidizes. Because you'll be drifting new paint on top of old, you want to minimize any problems that interfere with making the repair as invisible as possible.

In order to provide the best surface for the new paint, sand down the primer with 320-grit paper. This leaves it rough enough to hold the paint, but the scratches are fine enough to be invisible. Of course, sanding leaves dirt on the surface, so you'll have to clean it again when you're finished. Go over it with wax remover to get rid of the sanding residue, and be sure to use two clean rags for the job. One rag is to apply and rub the cleaner, and the other one is to wipe it off and dry the surface.

Once all this is done, you're ready to start dealing with the paint you've bought. The work area has been cleaned and the rest of the car has been either masked off with tape and paper or covered with large plastic sheets. Because dust is the primary enemy of a nice finish, you should clean up the area surrounding the car. The act of painting will tend to make the air move and, when that happens, dust is going to move around as well. The cleaner and more dust-free the area in which you're working, the less work you'll have to do later to clean off the paint.

MIXING THE PAINT

It might seem a bit funny, but actually putting the paint on the car is the easiest part of the operation. That's not to say that you can be entirely carefree about how you go about spraying paint. Just as with the other parts of the repair, there are many ways to mess up and, if you're not thinking about what you're doing, you can cause as much damage with the paint as you could earlier in the repair process. There's always a way to mess up if you really put your mind to it.

The paint has to be stirred every time you use it, and it has to be shaken well when you first get it. The pigment in auto paint is heavier than in most other paints and this is especially true for any of the metallic colors. A can that's been sitting around the store for a while will undoubtedly have all the heavy pigment at the bottom and the lighter carriers and dryers at the top. It's almost impossible to completely mix the paint by hand, so body shops have machines designed just for this purpose. Most paint stores have a shaker behind the counter and, if you ask them, they'll put your paint on the machine and shake it for you.

When you're ready to use the paint, the first step is to open up the paint can and stir it with one of the clean sticks you got at the paint store. Even if you had the can shaken at the store only an hour or so beforehand, there's always a chance that the heavier pigments have started to settle at the bottom. The level of the paint is probably close to the top of the can, so stir it gently. It shouldn't take a lot of time to get the color uniform, but you can't call it ready to use until you can scrape the stick along the bottom of the can and not come up with some gunk on the stick.

Once you're satisfied that the paint is well mixed, you can pour the amount of paint you want to use into a clean container. This can be anything from a few drops to enough for the whole job—it all depends on the equipment you're using to get the paint on the car.

A regular spray gun has a container that holds about a pint or so of paint, but don't forget that the paint has to be thinned before it's applied. The

Fig. 5-9   Before you start to paint, the surface has to be cleaned and the masking paper should be carefully examined for rips and tears.

arithmetic is minimal, but if you're going to thin the paint out by 50%, remember that you'll only need enough paint to fill half the container. A simple thing, but even simple things have to be remembered.

If you want to get a rough idea of how close the color of the new paint is to the old paint, put a drop of the unthinned paint on your finger and put it on the car. A perfect place for this is on the old paint you intend to cover with new paint. Keep a clean rag handy to wipe it off when you're finished. Don't be too worried if the color seems slightly different. The paint is designed to be sprayed, not dabbed.

The color of paint will change as you apply it, just as the color changes throughout the lifetime of the paint. The paint you're dripping on the surface now is still wet. The color and intensity will change as it dries and will change again when you polish it. Which way the change will go—lighter or darker—depends on the particular type of paint you have and other factors, such as whether you'll be covering it with a clear coat.

If you're afraid there's going to be a real mismatch in color, you can add other colors to the paint before you thin it and apply it to the surface. Body shops do this sort of thing all the time, but keep in mind that the people doing this have much more experience. Mixing and correcting colors is an art. Knowing which color to add and how much of it to use is something you can't get from a book; it has to be learned. Not only that, but because the color of the wet paint is going to change when it dries, you also have to be familiar with the paint itself.

Trying to do color corrections to the paint before any of it has been put on the surface is an iffy business, and you're probably better off forgetting about it. If you have a real suspicion that there's a major difference between the color of the car and the color in the can, you can prime a piece of cardboard and spray it with some of the new paint when it's dry. When the paint dries, compare it to the color of the old paint on the car. Keep in mind that you can't do really fine color corrections based on this comparison—the new paint will continue to change color as it dries further, over a period of weeks, and after the final polishing. All you'll be able to see by holding the painted cardboard to the car is a major discrepancy between the colors.

If you're absolutely, positively, certain you're facing a real disaster, wait until the first few coats are on the car and dry before you start mixing your own color. It will give you a better idea of the paint's final color and you'll be able to see if the mismatch is noticeable across the area where the old and new paint have been drifted. Remember, once you start playing around with the color, you're going to get further and further away from the color you bought and the formula used to mix it. Because problems even show up when colors are being matched by the book, straying away from the standard will only make things more difficult.

As I mentioned earlier, matching color takes a lot of experience because of the way paint color changes as it ages, especially in the first few months after it's applied. The best way to solve color mismatching problems is to buy the right shade of paint in the first place by taking a sample of the old color to the paint store, as we discussed earlier in this chapter.

Before you mix the paint you put in the container with thinner, you need to strain it through the paper filter. No matter how careful you are about pouring and mixing paint, there's always a possibility of getting dust and dirt in it, which will cause a lot of problems when you start polishing the paint. Even paint right from the can might contain solid residue, it might have begun to skin over while still on the shelf, or dirt may have gotten in while you were opening the can. Such things happen all the time and, since you've come so far and done so much work to reach this point, it would be silly not to guard against dirt.

PAINTING THE CAR

Now the only thing left to do is to get the thinned paint on the car. The work area, and just about everything else around, is protected by paper and plastic and, if you're smart, you've protected yourself as well. The dryers in the paint

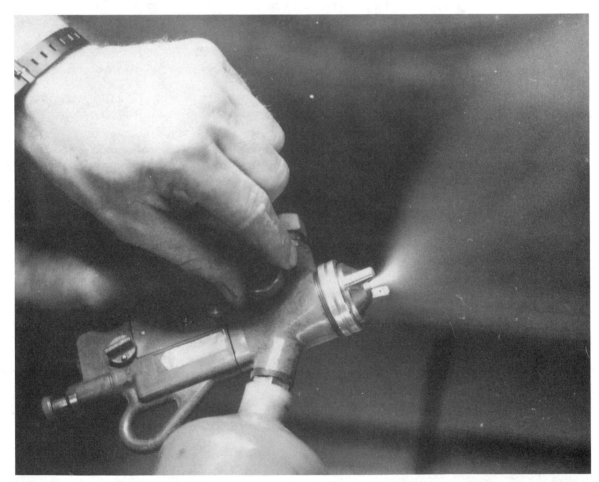

Fig. 5-10 An air-driven paint gun is the best way to get the paint on the car. The spray can be adjusted and controlled to match the job at hand. If at all possible, this is the way to do the job. The necessary equipment can be rented as well as purchased.

and the thinner can do really nasty things to your lungs, so it's a good idea to wear a breathing mask while you paint the car. You can buy these at the same place you bought the paint or at most hardware stores. If you're using a regular spray gun to put the paint on the car, you might give some thought to covering your hair and clothing, too. The very fine droplets of paint you're throwing at the car don't all wind up on the car, some of them get caught in the air and float around just looking for a place to land. After all, why else do you think you covered everything?

The only way to get the paint on the car is to spray it on. That's the truth. No matter how accomplished an artist you are or what you do to the paint, there's no way you can brush it on and wind up with a smooth coat. Brush marks always show up. Automotive paint is a heavy liquid that dries fairly quickly and, as a result, there's not enough time for the surface to smooth over.

The best way to apply the paint is with an air compressor and a spray gun designed specifically for use with automotive paint. This can be an expensive purchase—especially for something you probably won't be using frequently—but you can rent the equipment. When you reach the point of applying the paint, it's well worth the time to see if there is such a rental place near your home. If so, they should have exactly what you need, and the time it takes to drive over and get it is much, much less than the extra time it takes to paint the car without it.

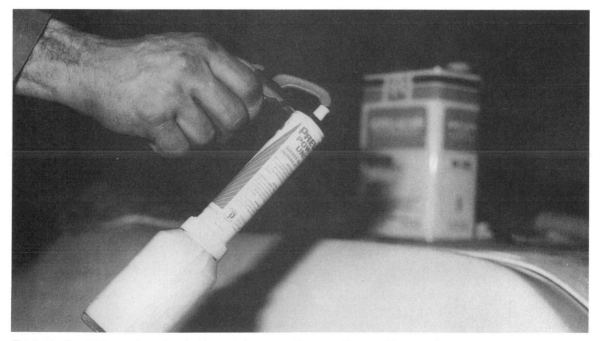

Fig. 5-11   Small jobs can be painted with aerosol sprayers. They provide you with a can of propellant as well as an integral container for the thinned paint.

Once upon a time there were inexpensive, pump-action hand sprayers designed for things like bug spray. However, I haven't seen them in years, and I'm not convinced they would work here—assuming you could find one in the first place. Some companies make automotive paint sprayers based around aerosol cans of propellant and, while such sprayers take longer than a regular spray gun, they work well and will put an even coat of paint on the car. The paint might have to be thinned in a different manner, but the equipment comes with clear instructions that tell you exactly how to prepare the paint.

You're the only one who can decide which method of spray painting is the most suitable and convenient for you. If at all possible, you should try to use a compressor and spray gun because this will give you the best results and provide a finished surface that's the easiest to polish.

Whatever method you use to spray the paint, be sure to follow the manufacturer's recommendations for all the equipment. The paint can will probably list how the paint has to be handled with various methods of application. Be sure to read all this stuff because the people who wrote it know more than you do and have already made all the mistakes you're trying to avoid. If you're renting equipment, spend some time talking to the people behind the counter. It's their equipment and they can tell you how to use it.

Once you have the paint loaded in the sprayer and are ready to put it on the car, aim the gun at something else and let off a few blasts of paint. You're checking to see that the paint is coming out in a uniform spray and that the nozzle of the gun isn't spitting occasional blobs into the air. If this is happening, check the instructions that come with the equipment to see what to do about it. Don't even think about aiming the gun at the car until you're absolutely convinced the equipment is delivering the paint properly.

Most spray guns have several positions on the trigger. Putting it halfway down will only spray air, and putting it down further will pull the paint from the container. Pull the trigger halfway down to make sure the gun is only spraying air. You're trying to see if any kind of liquid is coming from the compressor. If so, it could be water that has condensed in the system or the hose, or it could be oil leaking from the compressor. You can't start spraying the paint unless the air from the compressor is absolutely dry. If you are getting some moisture with the air, check with the instructions or the rental house to see how to correct it.

When you begin spraying the car, remember to keep the gun moving across the surface at all times. Just as you did with the primer, the idea is to build up several thin coats instead of one thick coat. One thing you don't want to see is paint dripping down the side of the work area.

Apply the paint in horizontal passes across the work area. Start spraying at one end and move the gun across the repair. Remember that this is the first coat, so you should extend each pass all the way to the end of the surface you're repairing and onto the paper or plastic you've used to mask off the rest of the car. The outer edge of the area you're painting is where you want the minimum amount of paint. Because you're drifting the new paint into the old paint, the periphery is where there is the least amount of new paint. The reason for going out to the paper or plastic for the first coat is that it's a convenient place to change direction.

Every time you change direction the gun stops moving for a beat or two and, as a result, you're applying a thicker coat of paint at that point. The periphery is the one area where you want to keep the coat as thin as possible, so you should do everything you can to avoid putting too much paint there.

Work your way across the entire repair, being careful to keep the spray gun in constant motion. When you reach the end, resist the temptation to go back and respray areas where you can still see the primer. Remember, this is only the first coat and you'll be putting several of them on the car before you're finished. Rest assured that the whole work area will be thoroughly covered when you reach the end of the job.

The paint has to dry before you can put on another coat but you needn't wait until it's thoroughly dry. The amount of time to wait between coats depends on the type of paint, the temperature, how much thinner you used, and so on. Again, there are recommendations on the paint can, but you shouldn't have to wait much longer than 15 minutes between coats.

While you're waiting for the paint to dry, carefully examine the surface for big particles of dirt that might have gotten trapped under the paint. You'll be able to spot them easily in the paint's shiny surface. If you see any particles, mark their location. You'll have to get rid of them when you're finished painting. This is especially true for dirt caught under the first coat of paint because the only thing underneath the dirt is a coat of primer.

You can get rid of the dirt after the first coat of paint has dried or you can wait until you finish putting the other coats of paint on the car. Because the dirt might get trapped on the surface as you put on the following coats, you might as well wait until you've finished painting completely. You can't just wipe the dirt off because the paint won't flow once it's been sprayed on the surface. Trying to lift or wipe off the paint will only result in a mess.

The safest way to remove the dirt is to let the paint dry for a day and then sand the dirt away with a very fine paper—nothing coarser than 1200-grit paper. This paper leaves the surface smooth enough to be resprayed with paint, and the repair will be invisible. Getting rid of dirt involves resraying the paint so it doesn't make any sense to do it after each coat of paint has been out on the car.

When the paint is dry enough to accept another coat, the procedure is exactly the same as the first step—with one exception. Remember to keep the horizontal passes further away from the outer edges of the work area to build up a gradually increasing amount of paint at the center and to create the area where the old and new paint are drifted together.

Continue adding coats of paint until the main body of the repair is covered well enough for the paint to have its full intensity of color. The number of coats you'll need to get to this point will be in the instructions provided with the paint and the spraying equipment, but it's usually around three coats or so.

After you put on the final coat of paint, carefully examine the area you've painted to make sure you haven't missed anything. Check the undersides of sharp corners and edges—particularly where lights and trim get put on the body—because these are easy places to overlook when you're painting. When you're absolutely positive that everything you intended to cover with the paint has been covered, you can consider yourself finished with the paint. If you have to put on some coats of clear, this is the time to do it. Clean all your equipment and repeat the entire painting process with the clear coat. You'll probably have to put on three coats or so—again, read the directions that came with it—to get a thick enough coat. The procedure is just the same as it was for putting on the paint.

When you've sprayed the last drop of liquid on the last part of the repair for the last coat, there's nothing left to do but clean your equipment and leave the car alone to dry. The drying times are listed on the paint can. However, because they can be affected by so many variables, it can't hurt to add 25% or so.

The next—and final—step in the repair is to smooth and polish the paint. How involved this is will be directly related to the kind of finish you want on the car. The smoother the finish, the more work it's going to take to get there.

For the moment, straighten up your work area, but leave all the paper and plastic on the car. There's really nothing you can do until everything is dry, so go outside and do something completely different. Forget about the car and the work for a while. It's taken a lot of time and work to get to this point, and you've earned a rest. Besides, you've got to build up the energy to finish it.

6
CHAPTER

Polishing the Surface

THERE'S REALLY NO REQUIREMENT FOR YOU TO READ THIS CHAPTER. YOU'VE PUT in a lot of work getting here. Now that the car is painted and the paint has had a chance to harden, we're into aesthetics, not necessities. The final appearance of the car—how smooth you want it to be—is totally up to you. The paint dries to a hard shine and, even though there may be some small specks of dust and other junk caught in the surface, the shine that comes naturally to most enamel paints is not too bad.

Not too bad, but also not great. And if you're using a lacquer, the raw finish will be dull.

No matter what anybody tells you about refining the finish on a car, there are really only two things to consider when you're making the decision. The first is how you feel about the appearance of your repair, and the second is how you feel about the appearance of the rest of the car. Before you decide what you want to do, you have to take a good look at the car, the repair, and what's on your schedule for the next few days.

Before you do any more work to the car, remember that the point of making the repair was to fix an eyesore. Even if the damage led to a severe case of rust, made the car hard to drive, or even left a trail of sparks when you drove down the street, when you looked at the car, the damage was the first thing you noticed. It's kind of like chipping a tooth—your tongue is constantly rubbing over the chip.

Just as something catches your eye because it's worse than anything else, something will also be noticeable if it's significantly better. Remember that the goal of the repair is to make the damage invisible. You really want the car to look as if nothing had happened to it in the first place, and that's what we had in mind as we went through the repair together. You matched the contour of the metal and the color of the paint to the originals, so you should take the same approach with the finish.

The first few times you do a repair you'll probably have more of a problem getting the finish to be as good as the rest of the car rather than keeping it from being better. Polishing a repair to a mirror finish might make your work look great, but it can also make the rest of the car look bad. The rule that you have to follow when you're examining the car once it's been painted is:

> **MATCH THE FINISH TO THE REST OF THE CAR**

Remember, the object of all the work you've done is to make everything the same as it was before the car was damaged.

Just because we'll be covering the steps you need to follow to put a brilliant, mirror finish on the paint, doesn't mean you have to take things that far. The repair work is ended when you can't tell where the new finish ends and the old one starts. And just as we did with the paint, you'll extend the polishing beyond the area you've repaired to help blend the new finish into the original one.

CUTTING THE PAINT

You'll remember that you took special care to place the masking tape on the chrome and trim when you were getting ready to paint the car. Now that the paint—and the clear coat, if you used it—is thoroughly dry, the time has come to take the tape off. Do this very carefully or you'll run the risk of lifting off some of the new paint with the tape.

You left about $1/16$ inch or so of chrome showing so—the laws of physics being what they are—you probably have some paint on the chrome right next to the car body. The only way to safely remove the tape is to cut it with a razor blade. Using a single-edged blade (and changing to a new one whenever it starts to get dull), cut through the paint along the edge of the tape next to the car body. The tape will be completely covered with paint on that side, and the cut you're making will let you lift the tape off the chrome without pulling the paint off the car. Dried paint doesn't lift where you'd like it to and many hours of work (and some exceptionally creative pieces of invective) have been caused by paint chips lifting off the car around the chrome.

If the tape does lift paint off the car, there are two ways to fix the damage. You can dab some paint in using a small brush. If you want to do things correctly, you can feather the edges of the damage with sandpaper, remask the area with tape and paper, and then respray with paint. These are exactly the same choices you have when big dirt particles get trapped under the paint.

Once you cut the line of paint, carefully peel the tape off the chrome, and keep the razor blade handy as you peel. It's easy to miss a few spots, and if that's the case, you'll need the razor blade to recut them. Lift the tape off slowly, making sure the paint is staying on the car. This isn't as silly as it sounds. If you do things too fast, you can create a few hours of extra work in just a few seconds. When all the tape is off the car, you'll have a thin line of paint on the chrome that you can easily and safely scrape off with the razor blade.

The moment you finish taking all the masking material off the car is one you should sit back and enjoy for a minute, no matter what you plan to do about polishing the car. Brush the dust and other stuff off the car, and just look at your work. Even though you might ultimately want more than just this raw finish, it still has a shine to it at the moment. The trim and other junk you took off the car to do the work might still be sitting in a box, but you're getting your first look at the results of your labor, and anyone who puts in as much work as you did deserves a few moments to bask in enjoyment.

Unfortunately, the few moments of pleasure you've awarded yourself to admire the car are more than likely a prelude to some more work on it. It's really rare to air dry the paint and wind up with an acceptable finish. Even if the shine and the texture of the paint match the rest of the car body, a close examination of the newly painted area will show you that dirt and dust has gotten trapped in the surface. If you rub your hand over the new paint you'll find that the surface, while appearing smooth, is really quite rough, and there are more than simple cosmetic reasons for curing this.

If a particle of dirt was sitting on the surface when you first put on the paint, it follows that there's no paint underneath it. And if that particle gets brushed or rubbed off the car, it's going to take the paint with it. One of the main reasons for taking the finish past the level left after the paint has dried is simply to protect the work you've done.

Although trapped dust is a problem on a newly painted surface, there are other reasons for further refining the finish. The quality of paint has improved tremendously over the years, but it still leaves a good deal of "orange peel" on the surface. This is an inescapable consequence of the way the paint dries, and even the car manufacturers haven't figured out how to eliminate it completely. Orange peel marks are caused by the force with which the droplets of paint hit the surface of the car. When they fall on the car, the impact forms small craters, and the paint dries before they have a chance to smooth out. When you get some experience under your belt, you can experiment with some of the paint additives designed to minimize orange peel. Most of them are chemicals that prolong the drying process, but they're not the kind of things you want to fool around with until you know what you're doing.

WET-SANDING THE PAINT

The best way to smooth down the finish and get rid of the orange peel is to wet-sand the surface. You don't have to sand the orange peel craters perfectly flat— that's a lot of work, and it produces a surface that's so smooth it might not match the finish on the rest of the car. As you sand the paint, you're wearing down the rims of the paint craters that make up the orange peel. The lower you get the rims, the less noticeable the orange peel will be.

The three things you will need in order to wet-sand the surface are sandpaper, a bucket of water, and a rubber squeegee to wipe off the water. At first you might have a hard time recognizing the pattern of the orange peel. Once you start sanding the surface and using the squeegee, however, it will become immediately evident. The sandpaper will first start cutting down the rims of the orange peel and, because you're scuffing the surface with the paper, the rim will become dull and the lower center of the crater will remain shiny.

If you are aiming for a mirror finish, keep sanding until the whole surface is uniformly scuffed up. It doesn't take that much extra rubbing to get to a mirror look and it does produce a more attractive finish. Remember, though, that just because it looks better doesn't make it the right thing to do. You want a finish similar to the one on the rest of the car. I've said this a few times before, but it's important enough to be repeated a few times more. It's just as bad to make things too smooth as it is to leave them too rough.

The basic procedure you will use to sand down the car now is much like the last step you took before painting the car. You have to sand the entire work area with a fine grade of paper and work your way over the repair until the surface is as smooth as you want it to be. The difference this time is that, because we're dealing with paint and not Bondo or primer, the abrasives you use are considerably finer than even the 400-grit paper you used as the final finish before the paint.

The roughest paper you should use to wet-sand at this point is 600-grit, but you're better off using 1200-grit. Choosing one instead of the other is a trade-off. The 600-grit paper cuts a lot faster, but it leaves much deeper scratches in the paint than the 1200-grit does. You don't need to take off much paint, so the extra speed you'll get with the 600 isn't worth the risk of taking off too much paint—especially if this is one of the first few times you've ever done body work.

There are papers even finer than 1200-grit, but most repairs don't need them. Keep in mind, however, that the kind of paper to use is also dependent on the kind of paint you used. As always, read all the instructions on the paint can and talk to the people who sold you the paint. If you still have some doubts, spray a piece of junk metal and, once it's dry, use it for test polishing.

If you run your fingers over a new piece of 1200-grit paper, you'll be surprised at how smooth it is. And, as you begin using it, the paper will get smoother and smoother. The idea behind wet-sanding is to dunk the paper in the bucket of water and sand the paint while the paper is dripping wet. After a few strokes, use the rubber squeegee to wipe the water off the sanded area and check the extent of your work on the dry surface. This sounds simple enough, but there are things to watch out for here as well.

The most obvious thing is to avoid sanding through the paint completely. It's pretty hard to do this with the grade of paper you're using, but it can happen if you get a piece of grit caught under the paper—it can be something that was caught under a piece of trim, something that was floating in the water, or even something in the air. Any of these will cause deep scratches in the paint. The only way to get rid of scratches is to either sand the surrounding paint down to that level, or to fill the scratch with putty and then repaint it. But let's take things one step at a time.

Cut the sheet of sandpaper in two and fold one part enough times so that it fits comfortably in the palm of your hand. Working the paper with your fingers as you wet-sand makes it easy to sand ruts in the paint, so always work with the paper in the flat of your palm. You can use a sanding block on any big, flat areas. However, I recommend using the palm of your hand because it will be easier to feel any grit that might be trapped under the paper.

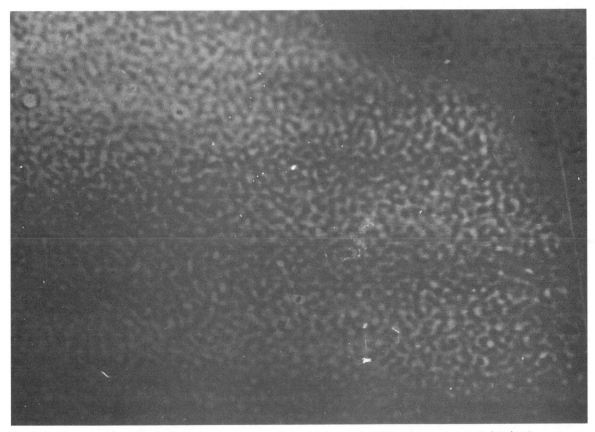

Fig. 6-1   The orange peel in the finish is caused when the paint dries before it has had a chance to level out.

Dunk the paper in the bucket and, while the paper is dripping wet, start sanding at one end of the repair, using circular motions rather than straight lines. Think of it as polishing, not sanding. Keep the rubber squeegee in your other hand because you'll be wiping off the water frequently to get a look at the dry surface. You can't make any judgments about how far down you've sanded while the surface is still wet.

Unlike the other times you've sanded the surface—and there have been a lot of them—when you're wet-sanding, it's not necessary to sand in only one direction. Don't forget that the big difference between wet-sanding the paint and all the other sanding operations is that this time we're using the paper to polish the paint, not shape the surface or prepare it for another coat of something else.

Because the wet 1200 paper is being used as a polish, it's also not necessary to sand in long strokes. As a matter of fact, you should move the paper over the paint exactly as if you were spreading on wax with a rag; use short circular strokes.

Don't begin by applying a lot of pressure. The paint isn't all that thick, and the one thing you don't want to do is sand it all off and get back to the primer. Go over the surface fairly gently for a few strokes and then use the squeegee to get rid of the water.

There's no hard-and-fast rule about how often you should wipe off the water and check the surface. A lot depends on the hardness of the paint, the amount of pressure you use, and so on. After you have a bit of experience, you'll develop your own style of working with the paper. In the beginning, it really pays to be safe rather than sorry. You're still getting the feel of how many strokes with the sandpaper equals how much paint.

The surface irregularities and trapped dirt that made the paint feel rough before you started sanding will begin to disappear almost immediately. The craters surrounding the orange peel, however, will take a bit more work. Stop and wipe off the water after every eight or ten strokes and carefully examine the state of the surface. I can't tell you how important this is, especially in the beginning. The only way to be absolutely sure that you won't go too far is to use light pressure with the paper and keep an eye on the work.

Because the surface will get scuffed up, it's difficult to tell when you've sanded enough off the orange peel to match the finish to the rest of the car. Experience will help, but for now just remember—it's better to take off too little, rather than too much.

You really don't want to be forced to repaint the repair. You can't ever be sure about matching the color, and you don't want to mask the whole car again. It's a lot simpler to take more paint off than it is to put more paint on. Trust me.

As you begin using the paper, you'll find that the more you use it, the more slowly it cuts the paint. This is because paint particles get caught in the grit of the paper and, together with the water, they tend to block the paper. The grit in

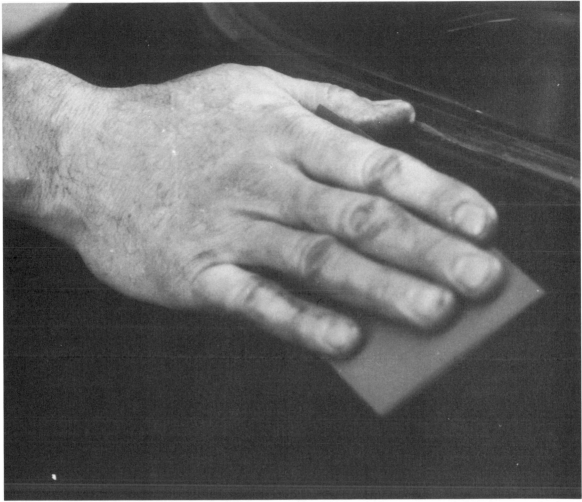

Fig. 6-2 Wet-sanding has to be done with the paper in the palm of the hand. Finger pressure is too uneven, and using a sanding block causes you to use too much pressure.

the paper will also get dull after you use it for a while, which can be a pain in the neck. In this case, though, it almost works to your advantage because it lessens the severity of the scratches left on the paint. You'll be cleaning the paper off every time you dunk it in the water, but there's no way to prevent the paper from blocking up or dulling. This is especially true with a paper as fine as the 1200-grit because the abrasive particles on the paper are very close together and the water causes the paint particles to cake up on the paper.

As you work your way across the repair, you'll undoubtedly come across places where it's difficult, if not impossible, to sand the surface evenly with the

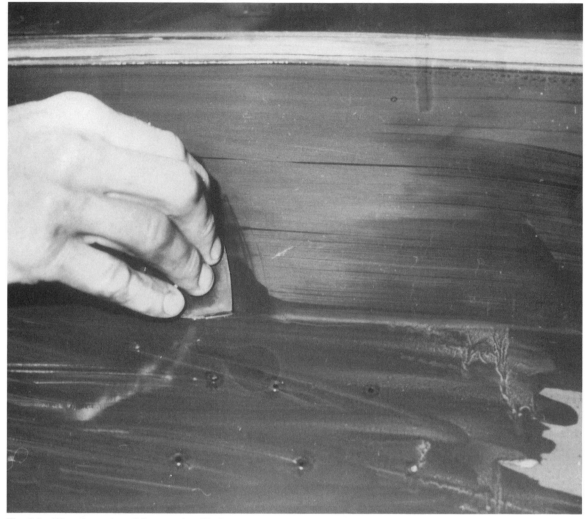

Fig. 6-3   Wipe the water off frequently with the squeegee to check the progress of your work.

paper in the palm of your hand. You'll find this kind of situation at edges, along sculptured lines in the metal, around lights, and so on. The only way to cut the paint down in these areas is to use finger pressure with the paper and bear down more heavily. Don't forget, however, that this is still a fairly dangerous thing to do because it's hard to control the amount of paint you're taking off the car. Get into the habit of wiping the water off and checking your work more frequently when you're doing things like this because you can't be sure of how much pressure you're using, particularly on corners and edges. You can always touch up the paint afterwards, but it's easier to be a bit more careful in the first place.

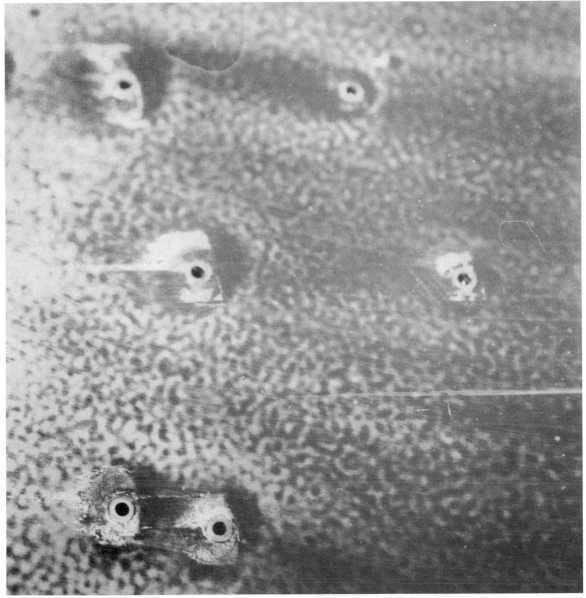

Fig. 6-4   When you start sanding the paint, the orange peel on the surface will become very evident as the rims surrounding the orange peel depressions get scuffed up.

Wet-sanding the paint is work, and there's no getting around it. There are other ways to do the job, but none of them can give you the same control or provide you with as perfect a finish. Unfortunately, it's also true that the only way to do it is by hand, so it takes a lot of rubbing and wiping to cut the repair

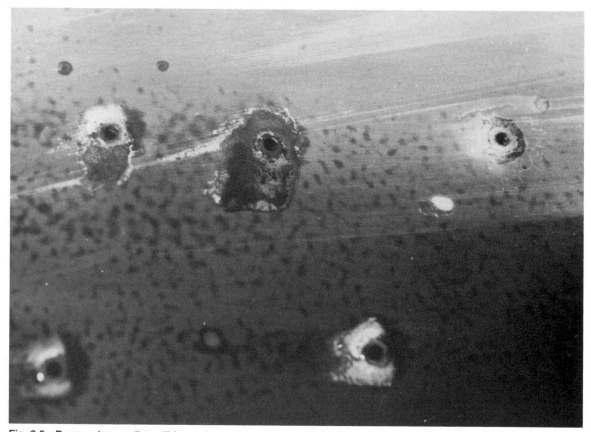

Fig. 6-5 Progressive sanding will lower the orange peel rims and make the paint appear smoother.

down to the correct level. Anything that involves repetitive manual labor like this seems to generate a tendency to speed up and cut corners as you get further and further into the job. Avoid this feeling. Giving in to it might get you through the sanding a bit faster, but that's only temporarily satisfying. Assuming that you're honest with yourself, you'll wind up unhappy with the job you've done and wind up putting in the extra time anyway.

When you finish the sanding, examine the surface under a good light and check to see if you missed anything. It can be difficult to get a good look at the surface. You might find it helps to have the light hit the surface at an angle, because that accentuates the difference between areas that are scuffed by the paper and those that are still covered with shiny, unsanded paint.

Don't go overboard in trying to be sure the entire work surface is scuffed by the paper. That will lead to a perfectly smooth surface and, chances are, it won't match the rest of the car. If you're not sure about how far down to cut the paint, pick an area of the old finish near the work area and sand it lightly to see how far you have to sand down the new paint. The size of the orange peel on the old surface will become much more evident and serve as an example for what has to be done to the new paint.

POLISHING WITH COMPOUND

It may seem hard to believe, but there will come a time when you have wet-sanded the surface to the point where there's a good match between the new and the old paint. It may take some time to get there, but that moment will arrive. The surface might look a bit messy, the water that's dried on the surface has carried with it loads of paint particles.

Wash off the work surface so you can do a final check of the paint. It's always possible to go back later if you find a patch needs a bit more sanding, but it's easier to do it now. The paper is out, the water's in the bucket, and you have a feel of how much pressure has to be used when you're sanding.

When the work surface is clean and dry, it's going to look terrible. The 1200 paper leaves sanding marks and scratches all over the surface of the paint. It stands to reason, therefore, that the next order of business is to get rid of the scratches, and that's exactly what you have to do next.

It's possible to get finer grades of paper than the 1200 we used to wet sand the paint, but no matter how fine the paper, it won't produce the kind of finish you want. The only way you can put a real shine on the surface of the paint is to use one of the many polishing compounds designed exactly for this purpose. These compounds are available in several grades, similar to sandpaper, but you should think of all of them as liquid sandpaper because that's really what they are. The main difference between the compounds and the fine papers is that the compounds can be made in degrees of fineness that would be just about impossible to produce in a paper. I suppose you could make a correlation between the grit of paper and the abrasive found in the compounds, but it's enough to say that the liquids are much, much finer than the paper.

Compounding the surface is usually a two-step process. The first time you go over the surface, you'll use a more abrasive compound. Then you'll use a finer one to get rid of the marks left on the surface by the more abrasive liquid—although it's really more like a thick cream than a liquid. If you find there are any very fine marks left by the final compound, you can buy a nonabrasive chemical to polish them away as well.

A tremendous variety of compounds are available on the market these days; a trip to the auto-body supply store will show you the truth of that. Of course, there's always the question of which one you should use, and there's no easy way to answer it. As with most of the work you've done, it depends on the chemicals and fillers you've been using so far. The best thing to do is to see if there are any recommendations on the paint can and, if you're still not sure, talk to the person in the store—he's undoubtedly been through this many times before.

USING A POLISHER

Once upon a time, compounding the paint was done by hand. You might not be able to understand how astounding a statement this is if you've never used compound yourself, but keep this in mind when you actually start rubbing down the paint with the first grade of compound. If you start to feel sorry for yourself because it's taking so long to do or it seems to be so much work, just remember the way things used to be not so many years ago.

In any event, most modern body shops use huge polishing machines to rub the paint down with compound. They are much like right-angle drills with large buffing wheels that do the actual work. They're also fairly expensive and, unless you plan on doing a lot of body repair, they're not the kind of thing you should run out and buy for yourself.

A reasonable alternative is to use a standard household drill with a buffing wheel attachment. A commercial polisher might take much less time to do the job than using a drill, but the drill will take a lot less time than a rag and elbow grease. If you want to get an idea of how much work it takes to polish the paint with compound, pick a small patch and spend some time with a rag trying to work the paint smooth with compound. No matter how much you like physical labor, hand-compounding the paint gives new meaning to the words tedium and boredom.

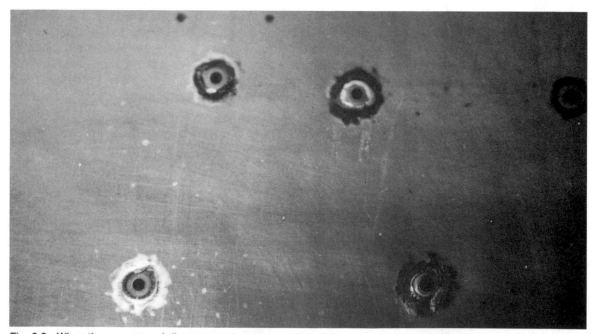

Fig. 6-6 When the orange peel disappears, the sanded paint will appear perfectly smooth. This is as much as can be done by wet sanding the paint and will polish to a mirror-like finish.

You can probably rent a commercial polishing machine and, if there is a rental place near you, it's not a bad idea to get one for a day or so—that's more than enough time to polish even a large repair job. Whichever way you decide to go, drill or polisher, make sure you have several spare buffing wheels. You can clean the wheel as you're doing the job but, sooner or later, so much compound is going to build up on it that you won't be able to use it any longer. As a matter of fact, it would be dangerous to try. As the buffer gets blocked up, it gets harder and starts to lose its ability to soak up the compound. When that happens, more and more friction develops between the wheel and the paint. This leads to more heat and, before you know it, the paint will be ruined.

The best way to clean out the polishing wheel is to use the tool that's designed specifically for the job. You can pick one up at the store where you got the compound itself. These tools look like a cross between a pizza cutter and a tool for working leather. If you don't know what they look like, ask the salesman in the store. As you can imagine, he'll be happy to sell you one—and he'll probably try to sell you a bunch of other stuff as well.

Fig. 6-7   The initial grade of compound will polish the paint, remove the sanding marks, and eliminate any residue of dirt left around the areas where the trim and lights are mounted on the car body.

The actual act of compounding the paint is very simple. You can dab the compound on the car with a brush or, if you don't have one around, wrap the end of a stick with a rag and use that. You will work the polisher on small areas at a time, so there's no need to smear the compound all over the entire work area. Follow the directions on the can, put a couple of smears of the compound on a portion of the work area, and start with the polisher. That's all there is to it.

Now that you know how to use the compound and how to keep it from damaging the paint, let's talk for a minute about protecting yourself from the compound. The polisher will throw lots of compound around, and not all of it is going to stay on the car. Of all the steps we went through together to repair the damage, compounding is one step that makes both the most dramatic difference and the most glorious mess.

Make sure you wear old clothes when you work the compound with the polisher. You will be very close to the work surface while you're compounding and—trust me on this—both your hands and your clothing will get covered with the compound being thrown off the car by the polisher. The best thing to wear is rubber overalls; they can be safely hosed down afterwards. Regardless of what you find to wear, rest assured that it's going to get ruined. It's not just that the compound is going to get all over it, the real problem is that the abrasive particles in the compound are going to get caught in the weave and, as you move around, they're going to wear away and finally destroy the cloth itself.

Using the polisher is hard work, and it takes experience to learn how to control it. It's a good idea to practice a bit on some junk metal before you start to work on the car.

Remember that the polisher and compound are removing paint—paint, you'll remember, that you worked very hard to get on the surface in the first place. One of the most common compounding mistakes is to spend too much time on any one area because the polisher will keep removing paint until there's none left at all. To avoid this you need to be systematic. Put an imaginary grid on the surface and do one square at a time. It's easy to spot places that have been underpolished, but an overpolished area looks just like one that has been done correctly. The only difference is that more paint has been removed, and that can cause problems later.

Work your way slowly across the surface of the repair, a small area at a time. As you compound the surface, it develops a real shine, nothing like the scuffing left by the 1200-grit paper. The compound makes the paint look very much like it will when you finally complete the repair. The scratches will disappear, and you'll be left with only fine swirl marks left by the polisher.

Keep the polisher moving all the time and carefully watch the paint as you compound it. The sanding scratches don't disappear all at once, and even a surface that appears shiny might still be covered with them. Remember that you're slowly wearing the surface of the paint down to the level of the bottom of the sanding scratches. Keep the work light close to the surface as you polish because as the scratches get more and more shallow, they get harder and

Fig. 6-8   The compound should be dabbed onto the surface of the car, not the polisher. The three dark globs on this car are enough to polish about one square foot of the paint.

harder to see. You'll know you've finished a particular area when the swirl marks become more noticeable than the scratches. The scratches can be hard to see—especially if they've been partially smoothed off by the polisher. Put your eye close to the surface and use a good light. If you let the light skim the surface at an angle, the scratches will be more obvious.

Just as with everything else you've done, it takes some experience to know when the paint has been compounded completely. And again you're better off doing too little rather than too much. Never lose sight of the fact that compounding means you're removing paint from the surface. If you go too far, you'll take all the paint off and have only a patch of primer.

Be extra careful with the polisher when you're compounding a corner or sharp edge, because the machine can easily burn off all the paint in spots like this. This is even more likely to happen if the polishing wheel is turning into the edge. Lift the machine so that the only part of the wheel touching the surface is the half that's turning *toward* the edge, not the half that's turning into the edge. If you forget this, there's a good chance the pile of the buffing wheel can get caught on the edge and the machine can go flying out of your hand.

Fig. 6-9   Keeping the polisher on an angle and using only one side of the wheel will make the machine easier to control.

Keep the polisher in motion and clean the buffer when it starts to feel gummy. When you can't get the cleaning tool to raise the pile on the buffer any longer, it's time to change the wheel. It's a real mistake and a false savings to try to get more life out of the buffing wheel when it gets caked solid with old compound and paint.

Obviously, you have to compound the entire work area, but it's also a good idea to compound some of the old paint as well. This tends to help blend the two areas, and the drifting makes the line between the old and new paint a lot less noticeable. You'll find it also helps to mask any slight differences there might be between the old and new color as well. Just as you did when you were painting, try to do whole panels. If this isn't possible for some reason, see if you can end your polishing on a line that's part of the body contour of the car.

Once you finish the initial stage of compounding, you'll have your first look at the completed repair. There's a bit more work to do because you still have to get rid of the swirl marks, but the shine on the paint will give you a good idea of what to expect when the repair is finally completed.

You'll find that the cream you use to polish out the swirl marks feels and looks more like a liquid wax than anything else. You can put it on with the polisher or, because it's so thin and the marks are so fine, you can rub it in with a rag. The choice is yours. If you decide to use the polisher, make sure to use a

Fig. 6-10 The small light-colored dot in the center of this photograph is a spot where the polisher has compounded away all the paint because the machine spent too much time in one area. The only way to fix this is to repaint the entire panel, so be careful when using the polisher to compound the surface.

clean buffing wheel, not one of the ones you were using before. The swirl marks will disappear very quickly and leave the surface with a finish that, if you judged things well before, is a good match to the finish on the rest of the car. Several brands of polishing creams can be used to get rid of the swirl marks left by the compounding. Check with the people in the store if you have any questions about which one is best for your use.

Keep the polisher in constant motion and work on a small area at a time. Most of the creams designed to get rid of swirl marks come in the same type of containers as liquid wax, and you can squirt it on the surface in the same manner. Keep working the stuff into the surface until the swirl marks are gone. If the cream disappears from the surface before the marks disappear, squirt some more on and go back to work.

You'll find it much easier to get rid of the swirl marks than you did to get rid of the sanding scratches. Even though the cream is much thinner than the compound, the swirl marks aren't as deep in the paint as the scratches were. There's a certain amount of poetic justice in the fact that the final step in the entire repair process is also the one that requires the least amount of work.

When you finish with the cream, the only thing left to do is wash and wax the work area—although it's a lot smarter to do the entire car. Because car wax is a consumer product, the array of brands available is staggering. It's a good

Fig. 6-11   The difference between sanded and polished areas is very dramatic. The swirl marks that are left by the polisher will disappear when the surface is polished with the final grade of compound.

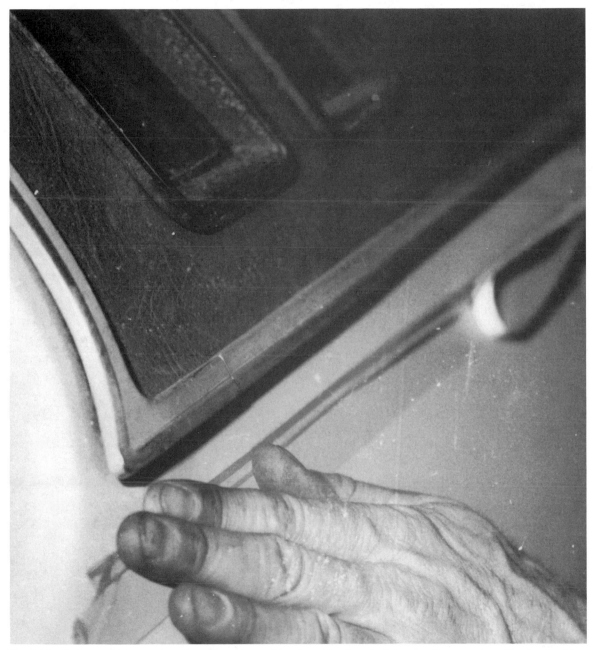

Fig. 6-12 Body panel trim can be aligned by using a strip of masking tape to determine the correct position for the trim. Lengths of body trim or pinstriping should be lined up along the masking tape to be sure it will be applied in a straight line.

idea to read the labels carefully because some of them are particularly designed for fresh paint.

You want to get all the remains of the compound and the cream off the car and, as you wash, you'll probably find some residue left from the wet sanding as well. Use a solution of soap and water to wash the car, and then rinse it all off with plain water when you're done.

When the car is dry, wax it with any of the commercial waxes—both liquid and paste wax are fine. Everybody has their own preferences, so go with the kind you're used to using. There's nothing special you have to do when you wax the car. The work surface can be treated just like any other part of the car. Most waxes have instructions that tell you to let it dry to a powder before you wipe it off. I don't like to do that because I've never been convinced that the dry wax residue won't act like a fine abrasive and leave tiny scratches on the car. You can do what you please, but I always work on a small area at a time and wipe the wax off with a clean rag before it has dried completely.

The very last thing to do, if you haven't done it already is to put the chrome, lights, and other trim back on the car. It goes without saying—but I'll say it anyway—that you should be careful while you're doing this. It would be a real shame to scratch the new paint, so take your time and check the alignment of the parts before you give the bolts that final turn or give the trim that final push. People have a tendency to get impatient when they near the end of a long job, and it's easy to mess up here if you rush things. It's taken a lot of work to get to this point and now, more than any other time during the repair process, it would be nice not to mess up.

PUTTING AN END TO IT

You might have a hard time believing it, but you've finally finished the repair. There's absolutely nothing left to do. Before you roll your car out into the light of day, you might want to check the polish on the chrome and make sure that the interior is clean. After all, you're going to call everyone you know to look at the car, and you've earned the right to bask in a moment of glory, as they *ooh* and *ah* from the side of the driveway.

This is the moment you worked so hard to reach, and it would be really awful to miss it. Part of the reason for doing the repair yourself was to save some bucks. But let's be honest here; just between us—lurking somewhere in the back of your mind was also how great it would be when you finished the job and it looked absolutely terrific. I know that one of the thoughts that kept you going through the seemingly endless hours you put in banging, scraping, sanding, and rubbing the surface was the moment of triumph that comes when you show off the result of your work.

As people come from far and wide to look with astonishment at the quality of your work, you can scratch your head modestly, look at the ground, and with a small smile on your lips, say the magic words: "It was easy."

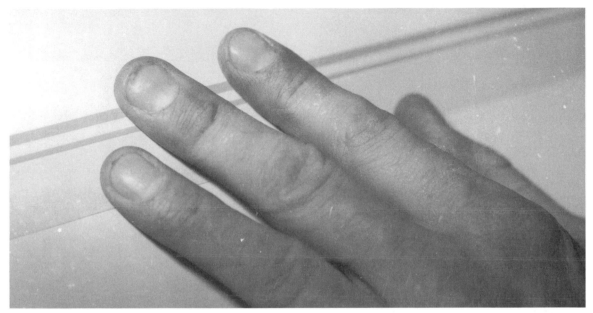

Fig. 6-13   Pinstriping should be put on by working on one-foot lengths at a time. Longer or shorter lengths are difficult to keep straight.

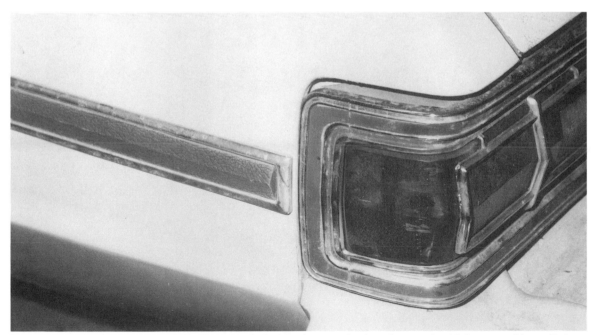

Fig. 6-14   The final repair, once all the chrome and trim have been put back on the car, should show no evidence that any work was done there at all.

Appendix

YOUR FIRST TRIP TO A BODY SHOP WAS PROBABLY AN EYE OPENER. AS SOON AS YOU stepped through the door, you were hit with a wall of noise and smells that were overwhelming. You probably made the trip in the first place because your car was hit, and your state of mind probably wasn't great at the moment either. That's all understandable.

But now things are different. Owning this book means you've got more than a passing interest in how body work is done, and a trip to the shop now should be instructive. I'm a complete believer in the idea that there's nothing you can't do if you really want to do it. Things that look hard or seem impossible only appear that way if you don't understand the procedures. All it takes to remedy that lack of knowledge is a basic desire to learn and a basic book to read.

Now that you're taking the time to learn how body repairs are made, you should take another trip to a body shop. The loud noises and exotic smells will be a lot more than academic. Spending five minutes watching someone work with Bondo or pull out a dent can save you hours of frustration. No matter how many words you read in a book, it's much easier to learn by watching. We all know the old rule:

A WORD IS ONLY WORTH A THOUSANDTH OF A PICTURE

It's really impossible to get everything down on paper, no matter how thorough you try to be.

Most appendices are lists of things in alphabetical order. This one is going to be different. The only reason I'm even referring to it as an appendix is because it's at the end of the book and it covers in a general sort of way, what you should know about the tools and materials you need to do body work.

Whenever you start something you've never done before, there's a real temptation to go out and spend lots of money on a bunch of tools and supplies you really don't need. There are very few tools whose sole purpose is to do body work. Most of the hardware you use can be variations on ordinary household stuff. While the ones designed for body work are obviously better to use, there's no reason you can't use their more humble, home-variety cousins.

Although the tools you need for the job are described in the main body of the book, we'll speak specifically about them a bit further on and indicate which ones you should buy before you get started.

You can be really creative about substituting tools, but the same can't be said about the materials you use. You can't do good repairs without using materials designed specifically for body work. The state of the art in plastic fillers, primers, and paint has gotten to the point where they're relatively easy to use and unbelievably strong. Several manufacturers make a large range of materials. They all do the same basic job but their particulars for mixing and usage are slightly different. The brand you'll find in your local store depends more on marketing than product quality so I won't make any recommendations for a particular brand. The best advice to follow is to talk to the people behind the counter. They know all the quirks of the type they sell—and all brands have particular quirks—so they're the best ones to advise you on mixing and usage.

TOOLS

The steps you go through in fixing a car—from pulling out the dent, to working with Bondo, to painting the metal—are each an art in themselves. There's just no getting around the fact that it takes a lot of practice to do each of these things well. You have to learn a whole new series of manual skills, and there's no substitute for experience. The same job you see done in half an hour at the shop is going to take a lot longer when you're working on your own in the garage. After all, you don't have the same amount of experience, and you're not working with the same tools.

There's no shortcut to gaining experience but there are some things you can do about tools. Hardware abound in body shops. As a matter of fact, you'd have to go pretty far to find a place where there are more special-purpose and exotic tools, each designed to do only one job. If you were able to prowl through a typical workbench, you'd undoubtedly find not only a collection of oddball, store-bought tools but you'd also come across a bunch of homemade tools as well. These are usually standard tools that have been customized by someone to do one particular job. You'd be surprised how many shapes can be ground on the end of a screwdriver or welded to a pair of vice grips.

There's no argument that the better your tools, the easier the job. But it's a waste of time and money to have your first venture into the wonderful world of auto body work be an expensive trip to the auto body store. You need tools to do the job, but not all jobs require specialized tools. Most of the work you have to do in fixing dents can be done with the kind of tools you probably own now. A few jobs, such as painting, just can't be done without the proper equipment, but most of the specialized stuff needed for these jobs can be rented.

Although a typical body shop has a bewildering array of exotically shaped hammers, a hammer is a hammer is a hammer. It comes in handy to have 10 hammers with differently shaped heads, but most of the work you have to do can be handled with a garden-variety claw hammer—the very same one you probably have hanging around your house. If the area you want to bang is larger than the head of the hammer, you can put a piece of wood on the car and bang that with a hammer. There's no point belaboring the obvious—if you don't know how to use a hammer already, you've got no business trying your hand at body work now.

You might find there's an occasional need for something heavier than your standard hammer. If you're into tools, you can spend the money for a sledgehammer. More than likely, though, you've got something around the house that can do the job. It's always a good idea to have the right tool for the job, but it's also smart to maintain the right sense of perspective on things. A sledgehammer, after all, is only a heavy piece of metal with a convenient handle.

Although we've mentioned using tools designed specifically for body repair during the course of the book, most are fairly expensive. Also just about all of them are air-driven, so you'd also have to lay out some heavy bucks for a decent compressor, hoses, fittings, and so on. This can add up to a lot of money.

When you come right down to it, the only time you absolutely have to have a compressor and special tools is when you're either priming or painting the car. There's just no other way to get the liquid on the car in a uniform coat. Brushes and paint rollers are out of the question, and even the electric paint sprayers can't handle automotive paint. If you want to do your own auto body work, you're going to have to buy or rent the compressor, the spray gun, and the other stuff that goes with it.

If you add up the cost of all the special tools mentioned in this book, you are looking at a serious number. Fortunately, as I've mentioned, you can certainly do some creative substituting. It's even done in body shops. The next time you go to one, a close look around the place will reveal old steel bed frames, odd shaped pieces of wood, lengths of two-by-fours, and other stuff that comes in handy when you have to do some selective banging or bending.

A lot of the air-driven tools can be replaced by the electric ones most people have around the house. I'm talking about things like an electric drill, jig saw, orbital sander, and so on. Air tools make the work go faster, but it's perfectly feasible to accomplish the same result with home tools. It might take a bit longer and you might have to work a bit harder, but that's the only difference.

Some general-purpose tools that aren't too expensive can make the work a lot easier. These tools can be used for things other than body work, so it's not hard for you to justify buying them. Pop riveters, rubber sanding blocks, and metal snips are good things to have around the house because they can come in handy for ordinary home repairs, too. You can get all this in the store that sells the paint and other auto body materials, but they're available in most good hardware stores as well.

Even though many tools you need to do auto body work are either things you already own or can make out of various bits of household junk, there are some tools that are specific to body work. The bad news is that there's nothing you can use as a substitute; the good news is that some of these tools are, believe it or not, inexpensive to buy—in the $5 to $10 range. This is particularly true for the cheese grater you use to do the first cut on the Bondo and the squeegee you use during wet sanding.

It's possible to come up with a substitute for the squeegee, although they only cost a couple of bucks so it's really not worth the trouble. On the other hand, there's nothing that can take the place of the cheese grater. You'll probably need several of them; they break fairly easily and get dull after they've been used for a while. You'll also want to cut some of them up and shape the ends to be able to cut the Bondo in odd corners on the car body.

The one tool that you're going to have to shell out some bucks for is the dent puller. You could try to improvise something with screws and a vise grip, but it's a lot smarter to accept the idea that you have to buy one of these. There's no other way to pull out dents from the front of the body panel without the risk of doing some damage to the car body. The only alternative to getting rid of dents is to bang them from the back side and that's usually impossible because modern cars aren't constructed in a way that you can easily get behind body panels.

Dent pullers are easy to use. Just thread the tip in the hole and gently bang the weight to pull out the dent. The key word to remember is "gently" because the metal in modern cars is fairly thin. If you pull too hard not only do you risk pulling the metal too far, but you can easily pull the tool out of the hole altogether. This means you'll strip the threads and the hole will be useless. Do this too often and you'll wind up with so many holes in the dent that there won't be any metal left to straighten.

There's nothing special about all the other tools used in body work. The pliers, screwdrivers, wrenches, and other standard tools you use are just that— standard tools. While it's necessary to have them around, it's not necessary to get a special set of them just for body work. And don't be afraid to improvise.

MATERIALS

As you skim through the pages of this book, it should become obvious that even a simple repair involves the use of a wide variety of materials. Each step of the repair process requires a different range of sandpaper grades, Bondo, and so on. Even if you do only a small job, you'll wind up the proud owner of lots of different tubes, cans, and jars of stuff.

This isn't any different than the collection you amass when you get into any kind of repair work. Doing plumbing or electrical stuff means you have to find room for half-empty jars of pipe dope, spools of solder, rolls of tape, and boxes filled with odd pipe lengths.

Most of the stuff you use when you do body work will keep for a good length of time if you do a good job of covering the container. Liquids like paint thinner and other additives will last a long time without any special care other than resealing the can well. Paint and Bondo will last as well but they do have more of a tendency to dry out. Fortunately, there is a trick you can use to make them last even longer.

When you've finished using the paint, Bondo, or whatever, spread a piece of plastic food wrap across the surface of the material inside the can before you seal it. Remember that the main reason a material becomes useless is that it reacts with air—either it will dry out, harden, or otherwise make the stuff useless. Even a well-covered can has air inside it, and covering the surface with plastic wrap will protect the material from the air trapped in the can.

There's not a lot to say about the materials you'll be using that hasn't been described in the appropriate sections of the book. The best instructions are those that are printed on the container. When you first get started doing body work, you should follow every one of the instructions to the letter. Developing the skills needed to do the work is difficult enough without having to worry about whether or not you've prepared the materials correctly.

SAFETY

Just about every paragraph in this book, and certainly every chapter, has been loaded with precautions. The stuff you'll be using for the repairs—both the tools and the materials—can be dangerous. Then again, the same can be said about most of the things you have around the house, so don't get the idea that body-working materials are things you should handle with a set of tongs while wearing a radiation suit. As long as you pay attention to the safety cautions written on the labels, you won't have problems. Most of these safety procedures are common-sense precautions you would take anyway. I mean, when was the last time you had to be reminded that the liquid in the paint can shouldn't be taken internally?

The major dangers in body work are assaults on your lungs and eyes. Safety glasses stop the flying particles that can get caught in your eye, and a breathing mask and adequate ventilation protect you from the dust and vapors produced while you're working. Even though these seem like basic rules don't be under the impression that they're trivial. It only takes one small speck of dust to cause a major eye problem, and the dryers in the paint can be very toxic if you make it a habit of breathing them.

Get into the habit of thinking before you do anything. When you're figuring how long a job is going to take, add another half hour to the time—that's 15 minutes to set things up and 15 minutes to clean things up. Most of the jobs you do during a repair, each take several hours to complete, so you can afford to spend the short amount of time it takes to make sure things are done safely.

Again, if you're not sure exactly what to do to minimize the risk from the tools or materials you'll be using, you ask the people in the store that sells the stuff you're using. If you have any doubts about how far to go for safety's sake, just go too far. To my knowledge, nobody was ever harmed by being too careful. The job will take a bit longer, but at least you'll be sure that you're there to enjoy it when everything is done.

Everything can be summed up in a few words and you should keep them in mind whenever you're working on your car:

DON'T WORK HARD, WORK SMART

The only pressure you should have to get the job done should come from yourself. Don't rush things. If anybody gives you grief about how long things are taking, just ask them if they want the job done Thursday or done well. It's your car, your labor, your tools, and—most importantly—your decision.

Index